Storytime Slam!

15 Lesson Plans for Preschool and Primary Story Programs

Rob Reid

UpstartBooks

Fort Atkinson, Wisconsin

Dedicated to…
***The Running Waters Poetry Slam Crew—Mike and Shannon Paulus, Eric Rasmussen,
and Ken Szymanski—for putting on the best show in town month after month.***

Published by UpstartBooks
W5527 State Road 106
P.O. Box 800
Fort Atkinson, Wisconsin 53538-0800
1-800-448-4887

© Rob Reid, 2006
Cover design: Debra Neu

The paper used in this publication meets the minimum requirements of American National
Standard for Information Science — Permanence of Paper for Printed Library Material.
ANSI/NISO Z39.48-1992.

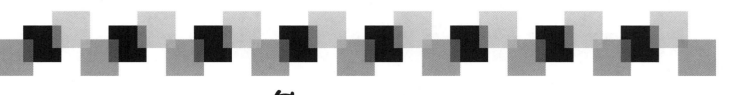

Contents

Introduction

I get a big thrill from making literature come alive for children. I do this through a combination of reading aloud, storytelling, poetry and wordplay, and musical and movement activities. The 15 lesson plans in this book are designed for 30-minute programs, but times may vary for individuals. Each lesson plan contains a few picture books and activities designed for heavy audience participation. Annotated listings of fun "Backup Picture Books" that fit each theme are included in each chapter. These allow for flexibility and take advantage of the multitude of great titles available on the children's picture book market. I have emphasized recently published titles throughout this book. However, to acknowledge many other storytime staples, I've added a list of "Old (And Not So Old) Favorites" in each chapter.

This was a fun book to assemble. Although I no longer work in a public library, I do visit several public library and school audiences each year. I would like to thank the children and their families for helping me hone my craft. I'd also like to acknowledge my Children's Literature students, many of whom become teachers and librarians, for their willingness to participate in many of the activities listed in this book. I would like to single out a former student and good friend—Zachary Fugate—for sharing his wealth of camp songs. Thanks to my colleagues in the College of Education and Human Sciences at the University of Wisconsin-Eau Claire for their support and encouragement. And a big nod goes out to the circulation staff at the L. E. Phillips Memorial Public Library, plus Gail and Cheri at the Indianhead Federated Library System, for "the heavy lifting" of what surely must have been a record number of reserves. Thanks to Michelle, Matt, and Heidi for inviting me into the *LibrarySparks*/Upstart family. And, of course, thanks to Jayne, Laura, Julia, Alice, Sam, and Daphne for being my center.

Enjoy the story programs!

B Is for Bulldozer

Heavy construction equipment and large trucks fascinate many young children. This story program not only features earthmovers and road builders, but the vehicles that travel on the completed roadways and the buildings created by the men and women in the field. Greet the audience members wearing a hard hat.

Picture Books

Dig! by Andrea Zimmerman and David Clemesha, illustrated by Marc Rosenthal. Harcourt, 2004. "Mr. Rally drives a big, yellow backhoe." He sets out with his dog Lightning on board. They have five jobs to accomplish that day: help build a bridge, shape a hill, clear a landslide, dig a hole for a new pool, and help build a new zoo. When they arrive home, Mr. Rally and Lightning dig in their garden for relaxation.

Monster Trucks! by Mark Todd. Houghton Mifflin, 2003. Each double-page spread begins with the chant "Monster trucks! Monster trucks!" The kids in the audience will likely join in with this chant. The trucks depicted include dirt-dumping trucks, garbage trucks, tankers, bulldozers, moving trucks, street-sweepers, forklifts, tow trucks, cement mixers, eighteen wheelers, and diggers. Each time I share this picture book with kids, someone yells out, "The trucks have eyes!" (They do!)

Musical Activity

"She'll Be Driving a Bulldozer"

Traditional; new words and motions by Rob Reid. Sung to the tune of "She'll Be Coming 'Round the Mountain."

She'll be driving a bulldozer
When she comes.

Push it back! *(Hold hands palm out and move them away from body.)*

She'll be driving a bulldozer
When she comes.

Push it back! *(Hold hands palm out and move them away from body.)*

She'll be driving a bulldozer,
She'll be driving a bulldozer,
She'll be driving a bulldozer
When she comes.

Push it back! *(Hold hands palm out and move them away from body.)*

She'll be running a big digger
When she comes.

Scoop it up! *(Make a scooping motion with hands.)*

She'll be running a big digger
When she comes.

Scoop it up! *(Make a scooping motion with hands.)*

She'll be running a big digger,
She'll be running a big digger,
She'll be running a big digger
When she comes.

Scoop it up! Push it back! *(Perform both motions.)*

She'll be working a dirt-dumper
When she comes.

Look out below! *(Cup hand around mouth.)*

She'll be working a dirt-dumper
When she comes.

Look out below! *(Cup hand around mouth.)*

She'll be working a dirt-dumper,
She'll be working a dirt-dumper,
She'll be working a dirt-dumper
When she comes.

Look out below! Scoop it up! Push it back! *(Perform all three motions.)*

She'll be on a cement mixer
When she comes.

Shake it up! *(Shake your body.)*

She'll be on a cement mixer
When she comes.

Shake it up! *(Shake your body.)*

She'll be on a cement mixer,
She'll be on a cement mixer,
She'll be on a cement mixer
When she comes.

Shake it up! Look out below! Scoop it up! Push it back! *(Perform all four motions.)*

She'll be steering a steamroller
When she comes.

Roll it flat! *(Twirl arms around each other.)*

She'll be steering a steamroller
When she comes.

Roll it flat! *(Twirl arms around each other.)*

She'll be steering a steamroller,
She'll be steering a steamroller,
She'll be steering a steamroller
When she comes.

Roll it flat! Shake it up! Look out below! Scoop it up! Push it back! *(Perform all five motions.)*

She'll be driving a street-sweeper
When she comes.

Clean it up! *(Make sweeping motions with hands.)*

She'll be driving a street sweeper
When she comes.

Clean it up! *(Make sweeping motions with hands.)*

She'll be driving a street sweeper,
She'll be driving a street sweeper,
She'll be driving a street sweeper
When she comes.

Clean it up! Roll it flat! Shake it up! Look out below! Scoop it up! Push it back! *(Perform all six motions.)*

Picture Book

My Truck Is Stuck! by Kevin Lewis, illustrated by Daniel Kirk. Hyperion, 2002. What happens when highways get potholes? A dump truck carrying a big load of bones (the truckers are dogs) gets stuck. Several passing vehicles stop and try to pull them out of the pothole. The rescuers are driving a car, a moving van, a jeep, a school bus, and a tow truck. The tow truck driver is rewarded with some of the bones, as are the creators of the pothole (which the kids in the audience will surely spot).

Musical Activity

"The Bus Is Coming"
Traditional; new words and motions by Rob Reid.

This version is based on an old spiritual, "The Train Is A-Coming," that can be found in Ruth Crawford Seeger's musical score *American Folk Songs for Children* (Doubleday, 1948). The kids can sing the "oh yes" part. As in many cases, when you don't know the original melody, just make up a simple tune on the spot.

Instruct the children to do the following activities:

Verse 1: *Shade eyes with a hand as if looking down the road.*

Verse 2: *Stand and line up. Hand each child a slip of paper. This is his or her "ticket."*

Verse 3: *Have them find a "bus seat." It doesn't matter if they are not in a straight row. They can sit anywhere in the program area.*

Verse 4: *Have them wave out their "bus windows."*

Verse 1

The bus is a-coming, oh yes,
The bus is a-coming, oh yes,
The bus is a-coming, the bus is a-coming,
The bus is a-coming, oh yes.

Verse 2

Better get your ticket, oh yes,
Better get your ticket, oh yes,
Better get your ticket, better get your ticket,
Better get your ticket, oh yes.

Verse 3

Room for many more, oh yes,
Room for many more, oh yes,
Room for many more, room for many more,
Room for many more, oh yes.

Verse 4

The bus is a-leaving, oh yes,
The bus is a-leaving, oh yes,
The bus is a-leaving, the bus is a-leaving,
The bus is a-leaving, oh yes.

Picture Books

Digger Man by Andrea Zimmerman and David Clemesha. Henry Holt & Company, 2003. A young boy loves to play with his trucks in a sandbox. He plans to buy a huge digger and "work while my brother sleeps." The boy plans to scoop up rocks and push mud. The boy's biggest dream is to build a park complete with a pond, a hill, trees, and a playground. The illustrations of the little boy in his hard hat on his big digger are great.

B Is for Bulldozer: A Construction ABC by June Sobel, illustrated by Melissa Iwai. Harcourt, 2003. This alphabet book is a good look at the various types of equipment, supplies, and personnel needed to construct big projects—in this case, an amusement park. Have the children participate by saying the letter featured on each page, starting with Asphalt and Bulldozer to the "Z-O-O-M!!!!!!!!" of the completed roller coaster.

Musical Activity

"Little Piece of Tin"
Traditional

The following camp favorite is a good way to end a program that features heavy equipment. This ode to a car that is on its last legs features the following motions:

Honk: *Tug on an ear for each "Honk."*

Rattle: *Shake head for each "Rattle."*

Crash: *Tap chin for each "Crash."*

Beep: *Touch nose for each "Beep."*

I'm a little piece of tin,
No one knows the shape I'm in,
Got four wheels and a running board,
I'm not a Chevy and I'm not a Ford.

Honk-honk, rattle-rattle, crash, beep-beep!

Honk-honk, rattle-rattle, crash, beep-beep!

Honk-honk, rattle-rattle, crash, beep-beep!

Honk-honk!

Backup Picture Books

Dazzling Diggers by Tony Mitton, illustrated by Ant Parker. Kingfisher, 1997. Anthropomorphic animals drive a variety of digging machines that heave, hoist, and haul as well as "crack and smash and pound," carry, lift, shift, "bash and crash and break, make things crumble, shiver, and shake."

Minerva Louise and the Red Truck by Janet Morgan Stoeke. Dutton Children's Books, 2002. Minerva Louise the chicken hops onto the back of a pickup truck and goes for a ride. She enters a road construction zone and thinks that it's "a truck farm." She believes the chute attached to the back of the cement mixer is a slide and that the crane is a big swing. When Minerva Louise returns to the farm, she sees a fire engine and states, "I want to ride on that truck next."

The Three Little Rigs by David Gordon. HarperCollins, 2005. Gordon's derivative variant of "The Three Little Pigs" features three tiny trucks that leave the safety of their mama's garage. The first little rig gets wood from a loader and builds a garage. Unfortunately, "the big, bad wrecking ball" arrives and says, "Little rig, little rig, let me come in," before smashing the garage to bits. The second rig makes his garage out of bricks with the help of a cement mixer. Of course, that gets knocked down, too. The third rig not only builds its garage out of steel beams, but also enlists the help of tall cranes that drop the wrecking ball and his mean cohorts into a melting pot.

The Trucker by Brenda Weatherby, illustrated by Mark Weatherby. Scholastic, 2004. Wesley is playing with his toy trucks when he watches the red semi-flatbed rig grow in size. Wesley climbs aboard and drives a load of lumber. He has many adventures including assisting a stranded yellow tow truck, driving through a blinding thunderstorm, getting a flat tire, and being rescued by the same yellow tow truck. Wesley wakes up to learn it was mostly a dream. The book includes a fun glossary of "Trucker Talk" with phrases such as "There's a Window Wash Up Ahead," which translates as "there's a rainstorm up ahead," and "Bubble Trouble," which refers to a flat tire.

Trucks Trucks Trucks by Peter Sís. Greenwillow Books, 1999. Young Matt owns several toy trucks and construction machines. As Matt plays, the vehicles grow in size until Matt is inside their cabs and driving them around. The sequence culminates in a double-page spread showing Matt operating a tall crane before everything returns to normal size.

Old (And Not So Old) Favorites

The Big Concrete Lorry by Shirley Hughes. Lothrop, Lee & Shepard, 1990.

Machines at Work by Byron Barton. Crowell, 1987.

Mike Mulligan and His Steam Shovel by Virginia Lee Burton. Houghton Mifflin, 1939.

Peter's Trucks by Sallie Wolf, illustrated by Cat Bowman Smith. Albert Whitman, 1992.

Truck Song by Diane Siebert, illustrated by Byron Barton. Crowell, 1984.

William the Vehicle King by Laura P. Newton, illustrated by Jacqueline Rogers. Bradbury, 1987.

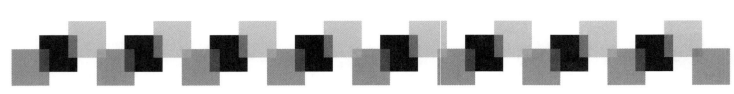

I'm Telling! Tales of Naughty Kids and Animals

There are many picture books that feature characters who are naughty, angry, or emotionally out-of-control. These stories can be very helpful teaching children how to handle their feelings. As the audience members enter the program area, play a recording of the traditional song, "Who Stole the Cookies from the Cookie Jar?" The song touches on the topic of taking things without permission and makes a nice programming "bookend" with the closing activity.

"Who Stole the Cookies from the Cookie Jar?" can be found on the following recordings:

- *Here We Go Loopty Loo.* Learning Station, 1997.

- *101 Toddler Favorites.* Music for Little People, 2003.

- *Silly Favorites.* Music for Little People, 1998.

- *Toddler Trio.* Music for Little People, 2000.

Picture Book

Sometimes I'm Bombaloo by Rachel Vail, illustrated by Yumi Heo. Scholastic, 2002. Katie Honors, like most of us, is a good kid. But when she gets mad, she's Bombaloo. She flashes her teeth, makes fierce noises, and lashes out, knocking things (and sometimes her brother) over. With her mother's help, Katie learns how to deal with her feelings. Sometimes, little things break her angry mood; like the time she threw her clothes around and "a pair of underpants lands on my head. Like a hat. When I laugh I'm Katie Honors again."

Poem

"Mr. Nobody"
Anonymous

> I know a funny little man,
> As quiet as a mouse,
> Who does the mischief that is done
> In everybody's house!
> No one ever sees his face,
> And yet we all agree,
> That every plate we break was cracked,
> By Mr. Nobody.
>
> 'Tis he who always tears our books,
> Who leaves the door ajar,
> He pulls the buttons from our shirts,
> And scatters pins afar.
> He puts damp wood upon the fire,
> That kettles cannot boil,
> His are the feet that bring in mud,
> And all the carpets soil.
>
> The fingerprints upon the door,
> By none of us are made,
> We never leave the blinds unclosed,
> To let the curtains fade.
> The ink we never spill,
> The boots lying round you see,
> Are not our boots; they belong to
> Mr. Nobody!

Picture Book

Rules of the Wild: An Unruly Book of Manners by Bridget Levin, illustrated by Amanda Shepherd. Chronicle Books, 2004. Kids have to follow certain rules set down by their parents. However, if the parents were animals, the rules would be different. Kids would be allowed to eat whatever they wanted, stay up all night, spit, splash each other, make loud noises, bathe in the dirt, chew with their mouth open, and burp out loud, among many other altered rules. Each double-page spread shows a different animal that matches the new rule. For example, the camel parents allow spitting.

Musical Activity

"I Wish I Were"
Traditional; sung to the tune of "If You're Happy and You Know It."

This is an old camp favorite with several verses floating around. I took what I felt were the "naughtiest" verses and added some movements.

> Oh, I wish I were a little hunk of mud,
>   hunk of mud.
> Oh, I wish I were a little hunk of mud,
>   hunk of mud.
> I'd go ooey and go gooey,
> *(Flatten hands on shoes as if spreading mud.)*
> Over everybody's shoe-y,
> Oh, I wish I were a little hunk of mud,
>   hunk of mud.
>
> Oh, I wish I were a little juicy orange,
>   juicy orange.
> Oh, I wish I were a little juicy orange,
>   juicy orange.
> I'd go squirty, squirty, squirty,
> *(Point to neighbor's shirt.)*
> Over everybody's shirtie,
> Oh, I wish I were a little juicy orange,
>   juicy orange.
>
> Oh, I wish I were a little mosquito,
>   mosquito.
> Oh, I wish I were a little mosquito,
>   mosquito.
> For I'd nippy and I'd bitey,
> *(Making flying motions with pointer fingers.)*
> Under everybody's nightie,
> Oh, I wish I were a little mosquito,
>   mosquito.

Oh, I wish I were a little striped skunk,
    striped skunk.
Oh, I wish I were a little striped skunk,
    striped skunk.
For I'd sit beneath the trees,
(Hold nose with finger and thumb.)
And I'd perfume all the breeze,
Oh, I wish I were a little striped skunk,
    striped skunk.

Oh, I wish I were a little bottle of pop,
    bottle of pop.
Oh, I wish I were a little bottle of pop,
    bottle of pop.
For I'd go down with a slurp,
And come back with a burp,
(Hold hand over mouth and puff up cheeks.)
Oh, I wish I were a little bottle of pop,
    bottle of pop.

Oh, I wish I were a little radio,
    radio.
Oh, I wish I were a little radio,
    radio.
I'd go click!
(Pretend to push a button or turn a knob on a radio.)

Poem

"Burp Poem"
Anonymous

Burp! Pardon me for being so rude.
It wasn't me; it was my food!
It didn't like to go down below,
And just popped up to say hello!

Picture Books

A Chair for Baby Bear by Kaye Umansky, illustrated by Chris Fisher. Barron's, 2004. Billed as a sequel to "Goldilocks and the Three Bears," this picture book finds Baby Bear and his parents setting out to repair the chair that naughty Goldilocks broke. The imaginative Baby Bear begs for a Robin Hood chair, a pirate chair, and a king's chair. The kids will have fun saying, "Please, please, please" with Baby Bear. Once at the furniture store, the Bears find that the Robin Hood chair is too scratchy, the pirate chair is too scary, and the king chair is too big and soft. They return home to find a package from a repentant Goldilocks who sent Baby Bear a chair that was, of course, "just right."

The Loudest Roar by Thomas Taylor. Scholastic, 2003. A little tiger likes to upset the peace and quiet of the jungle by belting out loud roars and startling all of the animals and birds. Monkey comes up with a plan to teach the tiger cub a lesson. All of the animals startle the cub with their own roar. Before reading the book, ask the kids to demonstrate how loud they can roar. Ask them to give the mightiest roar when you cue them.

Who Took the Cookies from the Cookie Jar? by Bonnie Lass and Philemon Sturges, illustrated by Ashley Wolff. Little, Brown, and Company, 2000. The storyline of this book is based on the traditional song. In this version, Skunk's cookies are missing. Skunk checks out the neighboring animals: mouse, raven, squirrel, rabbit, turtle, raccoon, snake, beaver, and frog, before learning that the ants took the cookies from the cookie jar.

Musical Activity

"Who Took the Cookies from the Cookie Jar?"
Traditional

Lass and Sturges's picture book contains wonderful directions in the book's front matter. Each child in the audience is assigned a different animal. The animals are accused of taking the cookies (and the child's actual names are not used).

Form a circle and hand each child a simple cutout of an animal to hold. The leader teaches the children the following pattern of lines:

> <u>Everybody:</u> Who took the cookies from the cookie jar? (*Repeat three times.*)
>
> <u>Leader:</u> Squirrel took the cookies from the cookie jar.
>
> <u>Squirrel:</u> Who, me?
>
> <u>Everyone:</u> Yes, you!
>
> <u>Squirrel:</u> Couldn't be!
>
> <u>Everyone:</u> Then who?
>
> <u>Squirrel:</u> Alligator took the cookies from the cookie jar!
>
> <u>Alligator:</u> Who me?
>
> <u>Everyone:</u> Yes, you!
>
> <u>Alligator:</u> Couldn't be!
>
> <u>Everyone:</u> Then who?
>
> <u>Alligator:</u> Bear took the cookies from the cookie jar.

And so on until everyone has had a chance to participate. Understandably, little children will have trouble picking up their cues and saying the correct lines. The leader can help them out by gently coaching them along.

Backup Picture Books

Are We There Yet? by Dandi Daley Mackall, illustrated by Shannon McNeill. Dutton Children's Books, 2003. A family of four (plus their dog) goes on a long car ride. The kids start complaining about the length of the trip. They are bothered by the fact that their parents are singing "Row, Row, Row Your Boat" and other tunes. Their dog's odor and their own upset tummies break up the boredom of the trip.

If I Were a Lion by Sarah Weeks, illustrated by Heather M. Solomon. Atheneum, 2004. A girl sits in her time-out chair because of her naughty behavior. She compares herself to a lion, a bear, wolves, alligators, and other fearsome creatures that behave worse than her. In the end, she realizes that the "opposite of wild is … me."

I Hate School by Jeanne Willis, illustrated by Tony Ross. Atheneum, 2004. A girl throws a fit at the thought of going to school. She claims her teacher is a warty toad and the kids are all tortured. Furthermore, the school's pool has sharks and "the sandbox is a soggy swamp." By the end of the book, the girl is sobbing at the thought of never attending her school again once she graduates.

Lilly's Purple Plastic Purse by Kevin Henkes. Greenwillow Books, 1996. When Lilly disobeys her teacher, who takes away her new purse "that played a jaunty tune when it was opened," she becomes very angry. She draws a mean picture of her teacher and slips it into his book bag. Later, she feels bad about her behavior and sentences herself to the "uncooperative chair." After she apologizes, she realizes that she really wants to be a teacher herself when she grows up.

Mrs. Piggle-Wiggle's Won't-Take-a-Bath Cure by Betty MacDonald, illustrated by Bruce Whatley. HarperCollins, 1997. This story is one of my all-time favorites and this picture book adaptation from the first Mrs. Piggle-Wiggle chapter book does a nice job. Patsy refuses to take a bath and throws a little temper tantrum. Have fun reading her lines, "I won't take a bath! I won't ever take a bath! I hate baths! I HATE BATHS. I haaaaaaaaate baaaaaaths!" Of course, Mrs. Piggle-Wiggle solves the problem with her "Radish Cure."

The Parrot Tico Tango by Anna Witte. Barefoot Books, 2004. The greedy parrot Tico Tango steals a yellow mango, a purple fig, a red cherry, a bunch of green grapes, orange papaya, and brown dates from the rainforest creatures. He loses them and watches as the other animals gather the food for a feast. Tico Tango apologizes and the animals give him another chance. "If you teach us all the tango / You can have a piece of mango."

Sakes Alive! A Cattle Drive by Karma Wilson, illustrated by Karla Firehammer. Little, Brown, and Company, 2005. Molly and Mabel are two cows that steal the farmer's truck and head into town. Several police cars chase them until they plow into the Mayor's flowerbed. The townspeople actually thank the cows for what they believe was a parade.

Old (And Not So Old) Favorites

Attila the Angry by Marjorie Weinman Sharmat, illustrated by Lillian Hoban. Holiday House, 1985.

Contrary Mary by Anita Jeram. Candlewick Press, 1995.

The Cut-ups by James Marshall. Viking, 1984.

Dinah's Mad, Bad Wishes by Barbara Joosse, illustrated by Emily Arnold McCully. Harper, 1989.

Goldilocks and the Three Bears by James Marshall. Dial, 1988.

The Grouchy Ladybug by Eric Carle. Crowell, 1977; rev. ed. HarperCollins, 1996.

Little Rabbit Foo-Foo by Michael Rosen, illustrated by Arthur Robins. Simon & Schuster, 1990.

Rotten Ralph by Jack Gantos, illustrated by Nicole Rubel. Houghton Mifflin, 1976.

Spinky Sulks by William Steig. Farrar, Straus, and Giroux, 1988.

The Very Worst Monster by Pat Hutchins. Greenwillow Books, 1985.

Where the Wild Things Are by Maurice Sendak. Harper, 1963.

As mentioned in the chapter introduction, there are many picture books available on this topic—too many to include in one lesson plan. Take a look at these other wonderful recent titles and consider them for your own version of the "I'm Telling!" theme.

Bad Dog Max! by Marina Windsor, illustrated by Steve Haskamp. Chronicle Books, 2003.

David Gets in Trouble by David Shannon. Scholastic, 2002.

David Goes to School by David Shannon. Scholastic, 1999.

Hurty Feelings by Helen Lester, illustrated by Lynn Munsinger. Houghton Mifflin, 2004.

I Am the King! by Nathalie Dieterlé. Orchard Books, 2001.

I'm Not Bobby! by Jules Feiffer. Hyperion, 2001.

Little Bunny Foo-Foo by Paul Brett Johnson. Scholastic, 2004.

Meaner Than Meanest by Kevin Somers, illustrated by Diana Cain Bluthenthal. Hyperion, 2001.

Mr. Wolf and the Three Bears by Jan Fearnley. Harcourt, 2002.

Naughty by Caroline Castle, illustrated by Sam Childs. Knopf, 2001.

Naughty Little Monkeys by Jim Aylesworth, illustrated by Henry Cole. Dutton Children's Books, 2003.

No, David! by David Shannon. Scholastic, 1998.

No Laughing, No Smiling, No Giggling by James Stevenson. Farrar, Straus, and Giroux, 2004.

That Makes Me Mad! by Steven Kroll, illustrated by Christine Davenier. SeaStar, 2002.

Too Loud Lily by Sofie Laguna, illustrated by Kerry Argent. Scholastic, 2004.

When Sophie Gets Angry … Really, Really Angry by Molly Bang. Scholastic, 1999.

Whoa Jealousy! by Woodleigh Marx Hubbard. Putnam, 2002.

I've Got the Blues

Many of the following stories and activities deal with childhood worries and fears. Much of the material incorporates color to convey these and other emotions. As the audience enters the program area, play Tom Chapin's song "I've Got the Blues, Greens, and Reds" from his recording *Billy the Squid* (Sony, 1992). The song's narrator sings about having the blues because he broke his parents' bed. He also experiences the greens (he's jealous of his brother's new bike), the reds (he's mad because his brother sold his skateboard), and the yellows (he's afraid of a bully). The song makes a nice transition to the first two picture books, which emphasize having your family to help you get through tough times. Explain to the audience that having the blues usually means that you are feeling sad.

Picture Books

100th Day Worries by Margery Cuyler, illustrated by Arthur Howard. Simon & Schuster, 2000. This book opens with the line "Jessica was a worrier. She worried about everything." Her long list of things to worry about includes losing her first tooth, missing the school bus, homework; but especially bringing 100 things to celebrate the 100th day of school. Her family comes to the rescue by assembling 100 different items from around the house to represent "100 bits of love."

Yesterday I Had the Blues by Jeron Ashford Frame, illustrated by R. Gregory Christie.

Tricycle Press, 2003. The young narrator has the blues—a bad case of the "go away, Mr. Sun, quit smilin' at me blues." He next experiences the greens, while other family members get "the grays," "the pinks," "the indigos," "the yellows," and "the reds." At the end, the boy appreciates his family all the more because he feels "all golden."

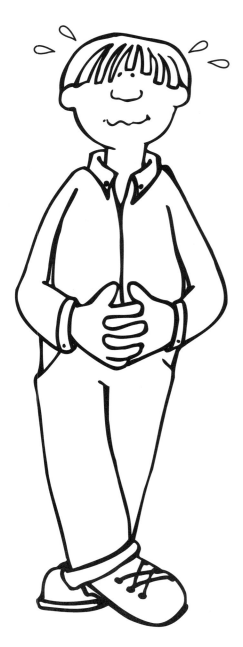

Musical Activity

"Shake Your Worries Away"
Traditional; new words by Rob Reid, sung to the tune of "Shake Your Sillies Out."

Direct the audience to stand and shake their bodies as your sing.

> You gotta shake, shake, shake your worries out.
> Shake, shake, shake your worries out.
> Shake, shake, shake your worries out,
> And wiggle the blues away.

The melody of "Shake Your Sillies Out" can be heard on the following children's recordings:

- *A Child's Celebration of Silliest Songs.* Music for Little People, 1999.

- *Country Goes Raffi.* Rounder, 2001.

- *Nancy Cassidy's Kids Songs: The Sing-Along Songbook* (with CD) by Nancy Cassidy. Klutz, 2004.

- *Raffi in Concert with the Rise and Shine Band* by Raffi. Shoreline, 1989.

- *The Singable Songs Collection* by Raffi. Shoreline, 1996.

- *Yummy Yummy* by The Wiggles. Wiggles Touring Party, 1999.

Picture Book

Glad Monster Sad Monster: A Book about Feelings by Ed Emberley and Anne Miranda. Little, Brown, and Company, 1997. This popular toy book features flaps that reveal monster "masks" that you can hold in front of your face to reflect the various moods discussed in the book. Yellow monster is glad, blue monster is sad, pink monster experiences loving feelings, orange monster is worried, purple monster is silly, red monster is angry, and green monster tries to be scary. The illustrations of the monster masks are silly enough that the kids will giggle when they see you hold them up in front of your face.

Musical Activity

"If You're Worried and You Know It"
Traditional; new words and motions by Rob Reid, sung to the tune of "If You're Happy and You Know It."

Ask the audience to perform the directions in the song as you sing. Exaggerate the different motions to keep the activity light-hearted.

> If you're worried and you know it,
> Hug yourself.
>
> If you're worried and you know it,
> Hug yourself.
>
> If you're worried and you know it,
> Then your face will surely show it.
> If you're worried and you know it,
> Hug yourself.
>
> If you're sad and you know it,
> Cry "Boo-hoo."
>
> If you're sad and you know it,
> Cry "Boo-hoo."
>
> If you're sad and you know it,
> Then your face will surely show it.
> If you're sad and you know it,
> Cry "Boo-hoo."
>
> If you're blue and you know it,
> Dance away!

If you're blue and you know it,
Dance away!

If you're blue and you know it,
Then your body will surely show it.
If you're blue and you know it,
Dance away!

If you're happy and you know it,
Clap and dance.

If you're happy and you know it,
Clap and dance.

If you're happy and you know it,
Then your face and body will show it.
If you're happy and you know it,
Clap and dance.

The melody of "If You're Happy and You Know It" can be found on many children's musical recordings, including the following:

- *Bob and Larry's Backyard Party* (Veggie Tales). Big Ideas Productions, 2002.

- *Let's Play* by Raffi. Shoreline, 2002.

- *101 Toddler Favorites.* Music for Little People, 2003.

- *Shake It All About* by Little Richard. Disney, 1992.

- *Toddler Favorites.* Music for Little People, 1998.

- *We All Live Together, Vol. 3* by Greg and Steve. Youngheart Records, 1979.

Picture Book

Aaaarrgghh! Spider! by Lydia Monks. Houghton Mifflin, 2004. A tiny spider wants to become the family pet. Unfortunately,

whenever a member of the human family spots the spider, they let loose with a loud rendition of the title phrase. The audience will have a great time hollering the same phrase. The illustrations are fun, especially the first page showing the spider's perspective from the ceiling that makes the humans appear upside-down.

Nursery Rhyme

"Little Miss Muffet"
Traditional

Little Miss Muffet,
Sat on a tuffet,
Eating her curds and whey.
Along came a spider,
Who sat down beside her,
And frightened Miss Muffet away.

Picture Book

Got to Dance by M. C. Helldorfer, illustrated by Hiroe Nakata. Doubleday, 2004. The protagonist moves to a variety of made-up dances in order to chase away her summertime blues. Have the audience stand and move while you read the book. The illustrations give clues on how to move to the various dances, but feel free to add your own touches. For example, when you read about the Penguin Dance, have the children waddle like a penguin with their hands down along their side. The tricky part is to hold the book, demonstrate the moves, and dance along with the children; but that just adds to the fun. Here's a list of the other dances featured in Helldorfer's book and movement suggestions:

- Grandpa Dance: *Move slow, but steady, and with a great big smile.*

- Raining-down Dance: *Hands start overhead, then fingers wiggling downward.*

- Every-Birdy Dance: *Flap arms like wings over and over.*

- Crosstown Dance: *Point fingers in zigzag directions.*

- Hopping-Hop Dance: *Hop around.*

- Boing-Boing Dance: *Hop even higher.*

- Upside-Down Dance: *Bend over with face looking upward.*

- Tap Dancing: *Mime the traditional tap dance.*

- Easy Ooze Dance: *Move arms and body in a slow, fluid motion.*

- Prowling, Growling, Howling Dance: *Arms upward and plenty of vocal grunts and howls.*

Backup Picture Books

Ish by Peter H. Reynolds. Candlewick Press, 2004. Ramon loves to draw, but becomes sad when his older brother mocks his artwork. Eventually, he gives up drawing until he receives praise from his younger sister. When Ramon says, "that was supposed to be a vase of flowers," his sister replies, "Well, it looks vase-ish!" This inspires Ramon to return to his drawing newly inspired. He looks at his art in a new light. "And Ramon lived ishfully ever after."

The Little Blue Rabbit by Angela McAllister, illustrated by Jason Cockcroft. Bloomsbury, 2003. A blue toy rabbit becomes worried when his Boy doesn't return to the bedroom. He and the other stuffed animals search throughout the house without luck. "Blue Rabbit felt empty inside, as if all his stuffing had been pulled out." Blue Rabbit burrows deep in the blankets where Boy eventually returns and finds him.

Llama Llama Red Pajama by Anna Dewdney. Viking, 2005. A llama child goes to bed, but soon calls down to his mother to bring him a drink of water. She's busy and doesn't rush right up. While Baby Llama waits, he starts to fret and worry that his mother may never come. "What if Mama Llama's GONE?" When Baby hollers, Mama scolds him for being impatient, but also reassures him that she loves him.

The Pigeon Has Feelings, Too! by Mo Willems. Hyperion, 2005. This board book format of the popular Pigeon won't detract from older fans. The pigeon complains that the bus driver makes him angry and sad. When the driver says, "Okay, Okay! You don't have to show us your HAPPY face if you don't want to," the pigeon goes nuts showing us how happy he can be. Willems's Pigeon books are a delight to read aloud; you can't help but convey the pigeon's emotions through the dialogue.

The Rain Came Down by David Shannon. Scholastic, 2000. The rain causes everyone to become moody and cranky, including the animals, the truck driver, boys and girls, and community members. At the height of this disruption, the rain stops and everyone's mood lifts.

Ruby Sings the Blues by Niki Daly. Bloomsbury, 2005. Both her entire neighborhood and everyone at her school complain when Ruby speaks in her extra-loud voice; all, that is, except for two musicians. They take Ruby under their wings and teach her how to control her voice. Soon, Ruby wows everyone with her musical talent. This fun story fits the theme under blues as a musical style rather than the blues as sad emotions.

Soggy Saturday by Phyllis Root, illustrated by Helen Craig. Candlewick Press, 2001. One day, it rained so hard that it literally "washed the blue right out of the sky" and onto the trees, the grass, the cow, the chickens, and the sheep. The eggs are blue, the cow gives blue milk, and the sheep gives blue wool. Bonnie Dumble was beginning to feel blue herself. She gets busy painting everything back to its natural color, including the blue sky.

Today I Feel Silly and Other Moods that Make My Day by Jamie Lee Curtis, illustrated by Laura Cornell. HarperCollins, 1998. The narrator expresses several moods including anger, joy, confusion, being quiet, excitement, crankiness, loneliness, happiness, discouragement, sadness, greatness, and silliness. The toy feature allows audience members to turn a dial to express their own moods.

Wemberly Worried by Kevin Henkes. Greenwillow Books, 2000. "Wemberly worried about everything!" She worries about Halloween, birthday parties, the cracks in the wall, "the noises the radiator makes," playground equipment, and mostly school. When she worries, she rubs her doll Petal's ears. She eventually meets another shy girl at school and looks at the world in a new light.

Old (And Not So Old) Favorites

Alexander and the Terrible, Horrible, No Good, Very Bad Day by Judith Viorst, illustrated by Ray Cruz. Atheneum. 1972.

The Biggest, Meanest, Ugliest Dog in the Whole Wide World by Rebecca C. Jones, illustrated by Wendy Watson. Macmillan, 1982.

Clyde Monster by Robert Crowe, illustrated by Kay Chorao. Dutton Children's Books, 1976.

Harriet's Recital by Nancy Carlson. Carolrhoda, 1982.

There's an Alligator Under My Bed by Mercer Mayer. Dial, 1987.

There's a Nightmare in My Closet by Mercer Mayer. Dial, 1968.

Three Brave Women by C. L. G. Martin, illustrated by Peter Elwell. Macmillan, 1991.

Just Ducky

There always seems to be a large supply of quality picture books starring ducks on the children's book market. Feature your favorites with an all-duck theme. Decorate the program area with yellow rubber ducks. Purchase a duck call at a sporting goods store and give a loud quack on it to shatter the quiet of the library and announce the start of this lively story program. Once the children have arrived, say "Let's get quacking!"

Picture Books

Duck for President by Doreen Cronin, illustrated by Betsy Lewin. Simon & Schuster, 2004. Duck decides that Farmer Brown must be replaced as the head of the farm. Duck wins the popular vote of the barn animals (21–6 after a recount) and becomes the new head. Duck goes on to become the governor (winning 300,002–299,999 after a recount) and the president of the country (winning 50,546,180–50,546,165 after a recount). Eventually, Duck goes back to his farm chores (mowing the lawn and grinding coffee beans) and writing his autobiography. Cronin writes very clever and witty lines that are fun to read aloud: "He gave speeches that only other ducks could understand."

The Pigeon Finds a Hot Dog! by Mo Willems. Hyperion, 2004. The pigeon from *Don't Let the Pigeon Drive the Bus!* (Hyperion, 2003) returns and "co-stars" with a duckling. The duckling wheedles a hot dog from the pigeon by asking a series of seemingly innocent questions and comments, such as "Would you say that it tastes like chicken?" The pigeon throws a tantrum, but eventually shares half of the hot dog with the duckling. Check out the subtle illustration on the back endpaper.

Fingerplay

"Look, Look, Look"
Traditional

> Look, look, look, *(Shade eyes.)*
> Three ducks in a brook.
> *(Hold up three fingers.)*
> One is white,
> *(Point one finger in one direction.)*
> And one is brown.
> *(Point one finger in the opposite direction.)*
> One is swimming upside down.
> *(Point one finger downward and wiggle it.)*
>
> Look, look, look, *(Shade eyes.)*
> Three ducks in a brook.
> *(Hold up three fingers.)*

Picture Book

Little Quack by Lauren Thompson, illustrated by Derek Anderson. Simon & Schuster, 2003. Widdle, Waddle, Piddle, Puddle, and Little Quack conquer their fear of water one by one in this counting/addition picture book. The audience can participate by counting along with the book's built-in "Quack-U-Lator." Use rubber duckies to help visualize the additions to the pond.

Movement Activity

"We're Going on a Duck Hunt"
Based on the traditional "We're Going on a Bear Hunt" and adapted by Rob Reid, after seeing kids play the "Duck Hunt" arcade game.

Have the audience members tuck their arms under their armpits to represent wings and practice waddling around in small circles. Have them repeat each line of the chorus after you. Begin with the announcement: "Let's go on a duck hunt. We'll pretend to be ducks so that we can get close to one."

Chorus:

We're going on a duck hunt.
We're looking for a big duck.
We have our wings and our waddle.
We hope we have lots of good luck.

Look! A hill! *(Point.)*
Can't go over it.
Can't go under it.
(Make over and under motions with your hand.)
We'll have to fly around it.
Flap, flap, flap, flap, flap.
(Make flapping motions while circling.)
We did it!

(Repeat chorus.)

Look! A town! *(Point.)*
Can't go over it.
Can't go under it.
(Make over and under motions with your hand.)
We'll have to waddle through it.
Waddle, waddle, waddle, waddle, waddle. *(Tuck arms in armpits and waddle in small circles.)*

(Repeat chorus.)

Look! A pond! *(Point.)*
Can't go over it.
Can't go under it.
(Make over and under motions with your hand.)
We'll have to swim on it.
Swim, swim, swim, swim, swim.
(With arms tucked in as wings, mime swimming by wiggling bottoms.)

Let's do a duck call.

Quack, quack, quack, quack, quack, quack, quack, quack, quack, quack!

Wait! What's that in the middle of the pond?

It's a duck!

Quack, quack, quack, quack, quack, quack, quack, quack, quack, quack!

Swim away! Swim, swim, swim, swim, swim!

Waddle away! Waddle, waddle, waddle, waddle, waddle!

Fly away! Fly, fly, fly, fly, fly!

Whew, that was close.

What's that?

Ducks aren't scary?

We should go back and make friends with the duck?

Okay, we'll do it all over again—tomorrow!

Picture Books

Mucky Duck by Sally Grindley, illustrated by Neal Layton. Bloomsbury, 2003. Mucky Duck is a white duck who enjoys cooking (pouring, mixing, rolling, shopping), playing soccer (dribbling, tackling, shooting), painting (dipping, sponging, squirting, splattering), gardening (digging, weeding, planting, sowing), and basically getting very, very dirty. The audience will enjoy chiming in with the frequent "Oh, you Mucky Duck."

Quack! by Arthur Yorinks, illustrated by Adrienne Yorinks. H. N. Abrams, 2003. Advertised as "written in the International

Language of Ducks," this picture book has no fewer than 79 renditions of the word "quack" scattered throughout the story (I counted them). Duck visits the moon in a rocket ship, quacking the entire trip.

Musical Activity

"The Quacker Choir"
Adapted by Rob Reid.

Allow the audience to contribute their own "quacks" by quacking along to any popular melody, such as "Jingle Bells" or "Mary Had a Little Lamb." Don't sing the words; simply replace "quack" for each word. Line them up as ducks and waddle out of the program area as they quack merrily along. This idea was inspired by those recordings of dogs barking Christmas carols every holiday season.

Backup Picture Books

Baby Duck's New Friend by Frank Asch and Devin Asch. Harcourt, 2001. Baby Duck accompanies a runaway rubber duck down a dangerous waterfall, through a scary forest, and into the ocean. Baby Duck bravely flies back, retracing his passage to rejoin his mother. The final line will make the audience chuckle as they hear Mama Duck say, "Tomorrow I'm going to teach you how to fly."

Duckie's Ducklings: A One-to-Ten Counting Book by Frances Barry. Candlewick Press, 2005. This clever oval-shaped book features several differently sized pages that reflect Duckie's search for her ten ducklings. They appear one by one behind Duckie when each page is turned. The kids in the audience will naturally see the ducks before Duckie does and they will holler for her to turn around.

Duck on a Bike by David Shannon. Scholastic, 2002. This silly story shows a duck finding a kid's bike and riding it all around the farm. The other animals have different reactions to the duck and the bike—most think it's silly. However, when a "whole bunch of kids came down the road on bikes" and ran inside the house, the animals each claimed a bike and went for their own spin around the farm.

Ducky by Eve Bunting, illustrated by David Wisniewski. Clarion Books, 1997. A toy rubber duck narrates this thrilling adventure that begins with a crate of bathtub toys washing overboard into the ocean. The duck dodges sharks and waves until it floats safely to shore, where two boys find it. The final scene shows the duck safe in a bathtub full of soap bubbles.

Guess Who, Baby Duck! by Amy Hest, illustrated by Jill Barton. Candlewick Press, 2004. Grampa duck shares his photo album with Baby Duck. She sees pictures of the day she was born, her first birthday, her "first wobbly steps," and more. Afterwards, Baby Duck draws a picture of a new memory—Grampa giving Baby Duck a kiss.

It's Quacking Time by Martin Waddell, illustrated by Jill Barton. Candlewick Press, 2005. Duckling is surprised to learn he came from an egg. His entire family is excited about the presence of a new egg in the nest. They all "quack" in delight. This is a very simple story, yet the audience members will enjoy quacking along in celebration of Duckling's new baby sibling.

Little White Duck by Walt Whippo, illustrated by Joan Paley. Little, Brown, and Company, 2000. This picture book is based on the popular song written by Whippo and Bernard Zaritzky. A mouse sings while the white duck, green frog, black bug, and red snake act out the lyrics in large, colorful double-page spreads. Read, chant, sing the text, or hold the pictures while the children listen to a recording of the song. "Little White Duck" can be found on the following recordings:

- *Animal Songs* by Phil Rosenthal. American Melody, 1996.

- *Burl Ives Sings Little White Duck* by Burl Ives. CBS, 1974.

- *The Cat Came Back* by Fred Penner. Shoreline, 1980.

- *Everything Grows* by Raffi. Troubadour, 1987.

Peep! by Kevin Luthardt. Peachtree Publishers, 2003. This picture book is similar to Yorinks's book *Quack!* in that a duckling and a boy say the word "peep" 33 times (again, I counted them). Once the duckling grows up, he switches over to quacking. The boy is sad when the duck flies off, until he hears a "mew." (There are 44 "quacks" and six "mews," for those keeping count.)

Webster J. Duck by Martin Waddell, illustrated by David Parkins. Candlewick

Press, 2001. This is one of the best of the countless farm animal noises books out on the picture book market. Webster J. Duck hatches and searches for his mother. Webster meets a "Duck with a Waggly Tail" (a dog), a "Big Woolly Duck" (a sheep), and a "Bigger Big Duck" (a cow). He knows by their animal noises that they can't be his mother. "My mother would go 'quack-quack' like me!"

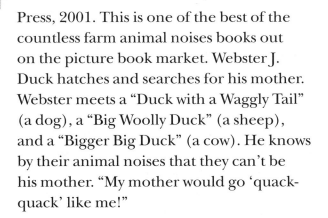

Old (And Not So Old) Favorites

The Chick and the Duckling by V. Suteyev, translated by Mirra Ginsburg, illustrated by Jose Aruego and Ariane Dewey. Macmillan, 1972.

Farmer Duck by Martin Waddell, illustrated by Helen Oxenbury. Candlewick Press, 1992.

Happy Birthday, Dear Duck by Eve Bunting, illustrated by Jan Brett. Clarion Books, 1988.

Have You Seen My Duckling? by Nancy Tafuri. Greenwillow Books, 1984.

In the Rain with Baby Duck by Amy Hest, illustrated by Jill Barton. Candlewick Press, 1995.

Make Way for Ducklings by Robert McCloskey. Viking, 1941.

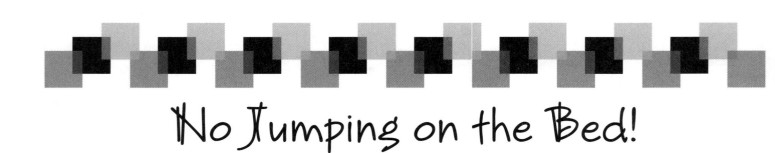

No Jumping on the Bed!

This chapter features storybook characters that jump, hop, and bounce. Sprinkle jump-rope rhymes throughout the program. Many of these rhymes can be chanted or transformed into movement activities suitable for story programs without the need of an actual jump rope. You can find many jump-rope rhymes on the Internet using various search engines or in the excellent print source *Anna Banana: 101 Jump-Rope Rhymes* by Joanna Cole, illustrated by Alan Tiegreen (William Morrow & Co., 1989).

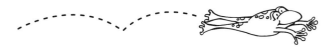

Picture Book/Fingerplay

Five Little Monkeys Jumping on the Bed by Eileen Christelow. Clarion Books, 1989.

This book follows the popular traditional fingerplay. Cartoon-style anthropomorphic monkeys give their mother fits by misbehaving at bedtime. By the end of the book, however, mama monkey playfully jumps up and down on her own bed. Here are the words to the fingerplay:

> Five little monkeys jumping on the bed,
> (*Hold up five fingers on one hand and move them up and down on the open palm of the other hand.*)
>
> One fell off and bumped his head.
> (*Hold head and shake it back and forth.*)
>
> Mama called the doctor and the doctor said,
> (*Mime using a telephone.*)
>
> "No more monkeys jumping on the bed."
> (*Shake finger.*)

Repeat the verses, counting down to one.

Musical Activity

"Five in the Bed"
Traditional; new words and motions by Rob Reid, sung to the tune of "Ten in the Bed."

There were five in the bed,
And the little one said,
"Let's all jump! Boing! Boing!"
(*Kids jump twice.*)
So everyone jumped and one fell off.

There were four in the bed,
And the little one said,
"Let's all jump! Boing! Boing!"
(*Kids jump twice.*)
So everyone jumped and one fell off.

There were three in the bed,
And the little one said,
"Let's all jump! Boing! Boing!"
(*Kids jump twice.*)
So everyone jumped and one fell off.

There were two in the bed,
And the little one said,
"Let's all jump! Boing! Boing!"
(*Kids jump twice.*)
So everyone jumped and one fell off.

There was one in the bed,
And the little one said,
"Let's all jump! Boing! Boing!"
(*Kids jump twice.*)
So that one jumped and he/she fell off.

There were none in the bed,
And nobody said,
"Let's all jump! Boing! Boing!"
(*Joke with the kids to jump twice anyway.*)

Picture Book

Emily Loves to Bounce by Stephen Michael King. Philomel Books, 2003. Emily has a knack for bouncing in several styles:

"… high bounces, low bounces, springy bounces, boinging bounces …" Emily also loves to bounce with different animals in different places, but her favorite place to bounce is on Mom and Dad's bed.

Jump-Rope Chant

"A Sailor Went to Sea"
Traditional

A sailor went to sea-sea-sea,
To see what he could see-see-see.
But all that he could see-see-see,
Was the bottom of the deep blue sea-sea-sea.
(*Repeat reciting the rhyme faster and faster.*)

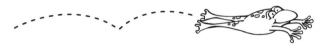

Picture Book

Boing by Nick Bruel. Roaring Brook Press, 2004. Mother Kangaroo tries to teach her child how to jump. The little kangaroo has trouble getting any lift-off. Other animals come along and try to assist. Finally, a koala has the young kangaroo empty his pouch. Kids will hoot at the hilarious contents weighing the kangaroo down. With an empty "pocket," the young kangaroo leaps with a big "Boing" in a large, two-page foldout spread.

Poem

"The Kangaroo"
Anonymous
Read while holding a kangaroo puppet or a picture of a kangaroo.

Old Jumpety-Bumpety-Hop-and-Go-One,
Was lying asleep on his side in the sun.
This old kangaroo,
He was whisking the flies,
With his long glossy tail,
From his ears and his eyes.
Jumpety-Bumpety-Hop-and-Go-One,
Was lying asleep on his side in the sun.
Jumpety-Bumpety-Hop!

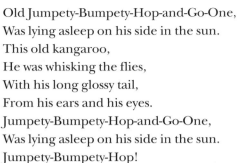

Song

"Grasshopper"
Traditional; sung to the tune of "The Battle Hymn of the Republic."

Ask the kids what other types of creatures jump, hop, and bounce. Suggest grasshoppers if they don't mention these lively insects. Have your audience members hold up two fingers while you sing.

> The first grasshopper jumped right over the second grasshopper's back.
> *(Move one finger "jump" over the other finger. Repeat actions after each verse.)*
>
> Oh, the first grasshopper jumped right over the second grasshopper's back.
>
> The first grasshopper jumped right over the second grasshopper's back.
>
> Yes, the first grasshopper jumped right over the second grasshopper's back.
>
> They were only playing leapfrog.
> They were only playing leapfrog.
> They were only playing leapfrog.
>
> When the first grasshopper jumped right over the second grasshopper's back.

Picture Book

Oops-a-Daisy! by Claire Freedman, illustrated by Gaby Hansen. Tiger Tales, 2004. This picture book features fun wordplay. Mama Rabbit tries to teach her child to hop. The hops turn into "hippety-hoppety flops." Mama reassures her child Daisy that "no one gets it right the first time." The two of them observe other animals. Little Mouse tries to reach golden seeds to eat and falls with a "slippity-flippety." Little Badger tries to dig a tunnel, but the tunnel collapses with a "crashity-smashity." Little Duckling practices swimming, but crashes into lily pads with a "splashity-crashity." They all turn out fine in the end.

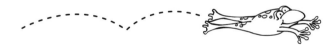

Jump Rope Chant

"Bubblegum, Bubblegum"
Traditional

> Bubblegum, bubblegum, chew and blow.
> *(Mime chewing.)*
>
> Bubblegum, bubblegum, scrape your toe.
> *(Dig toe into floor.)*
>
> Bubblegum, bubblegum, tastes so sweet.
> *(Rub belly.)*
>
> Get that bubblegum off your feet!
> *(Mime sticky feet.)*

Picture Book

McGillycuddy Could! by Pamela Duncan Edwards, illustrated by Sue Porter. HarperCollins, 2005. A kangaroo arrives at a farm and demonstrates how he can hop, jump, bounce, and kick. After the various farm animals ask him if he can make milk, grow wool, lay eggs, or cock-a-doodle-doo, he feels inadequate and leaves. He returns in time to save the day when he hops, jumps, bounces, and kicks a marauding fox.

Jump Rope Chant

"Oliver Twist"
Traditional

Finish the program with this movement activity based on the traditional jump-rope rhyme. Before you recite the chant, demonstrate tiny "kicks" and "twists," so the kids won't get too carried away.

> Oliver jump,
> Oliver jump, jump, jump.
> Oliver kick,
> Oliver kick, kick, kick.
> Oliver twist,
> Oliver twist, twist, twist.
> Oliver jump jump jump.
> Oliver kick kick kick.
> Oliver twist twist twist.

Backup Picture Books

Do Donkeys Dance? by Melanie Walsh. Houghton Mifflin, 2000. Kids are asked a series of questions accompanied by silly pictures. Do turtles leap? No, kangaroos do. Do hippos hop? No, fleas hop. The kids will have fun supplying the correct answers. The book ends with a surprise.

Naughty Little Monkeys by Jim Aylesworth, illustrated by Henry Cole. Dutton Children's Books, 2003. Twenty-six monkeys jump around after bedtime. They run through an alphabetical litany of naughty escapades. Their parents return home to find a mess similar to the chaos found in Eileen Christelow's Five Little Monkeys books.

Read-Aloud Rhymes for the Very Young by Jack Prelutsky, illustrated by Marc Brown. Knopf, 1986. Read the poem "Somersaults." The narrator turns somersaults, bounces on the bed, swings like a monkey, hops like a rabbit, leaps like a frog, jumps like a flea, and concludes with "there must be rubber inside of me."

The Teeny Weeny Tadpole by Sheridan Cain, illustrated by Jack Tickle. Tiger Tales, 2005. Tadpole wishes he could leap like Mommy Frog, Lamb, Rabbit, and Grasshopper. By the time Big Bad Fish gives chase, Teeny Weeny Tadpole has transformed into Little Frog and jumps higher than all of the other animals.

The Very Boastful Kangaroo by Bernard Most. Harcourt, 1999. This story is basically a joke turned into a cute little easy reader book. Kangaroo is boastful about his jumping abilities. A teeny, tiny kangaroo sets up a challenge to jump higher than a tall tree. The teeny, tiny kangaroo jumps a "teeny, tiny jump" and wins because "trees can't jump."

You Read to Me, I'll Read to You by Mary Ann Hoberman, illustrated by Michael Emberley. Little, Brown, and Company,

2004. Read the poem "Hop and Skip." Have a companion read this piece with you as this book is designed for two voices. One reader likes to hop; the other likes to skip. Sometimes they trip and slip and other times it's nice to stop and read.

Old (And Not So Old) Favorites

Hop Jump by Ellen Stoll Walsh. Harcourt, 1993.

Hop on Pop by Dr. Seuss. Random House, 1963.

I Made a Mistake: Based on a Jump Rope Rhyme by Miriam Nerlove. Atheneum, 1985.

Joey by Jack Kent. Prentice-Hall, 1984.

Joey Runs Away by Jack Kent. Prentice-Hall, 1985.

Jump Frog Jump by Robert Kalan, illustrated by Byron Barton. Greenwillow Books, 1981.

Katy No Pocket by Emmy Payne. Houghton Mifflin, 1944.

Mrs. Mooley by Jack Kent. Golden Books, 1973.

No Jumping on the Bed! by Tedd Arnold. Dial, 1987.

No Moon, No Milk! by Chris Babcock, illustrated by Mark Teague. Crown Publishers, 1993.

Norma Jean, Jumping Bean by Joanna Cole, illustrated by Lynn Munsinger. Random House, 1987.

Splash! by Ann Jonas. Greenwillow Books, 1995.

More Fun Jump-Rope Chants

"Alice, Where Are You Going?"
Traditional

Alice, where are you going?
Upstairs to take a bath.
Alice, with legs like toothpicks and a neck like a giraffe-affe-affe-affe.
Alice, up in the bathtub,
Alice pulled the plug. Two, three, four.
Oh, my goodness! Oh, my soul!
There goes Alice down the hole!
Glub glub glub glub glub!

"I Asked My Mother."
Traditional

I asked my mother for fifty cents,
To see an elephant jump the fence.
He jumped so high that he touched the sky,
And didn't come back till the Fourth of July.

"Jelly in the Dish."
Traditional; this jump-rope chant can be used as a simple, short movement stretcher between stories.

Jelly in the dish.
Jelly in the dish.
Wiggle waggle wiggle waggle,
Jelly in the dish.

"Lemonade, Crunchy Ice"
Traditional; have children stand, move in place, turn around, touch the ground, then freeze in place at the end.

Lemonade, crunchy ice,
Beat it once, beat it twice.
Lemonade, crunchy ice,
Beat it once, beat it twice.

Turn around, touch the ground, and FREEZE!

Oh, No! Stories and Activities that Feature the Letter "O"

This type of theme is particularly fun to put together. It's very similar to a scavenger hunt to locate material. Search for "O" words in the dictionary and conduct keyword searches on the library's online catalog of names that start with the letter "O." You can do this with any letter of the alphabet to develop a fun theme that gives you a lot of flexibility. As the children enter the program area, play a recording of *"Octopus's Garden"* by The Beatles from the recording *Abbey Road* (Apple, 1969). This song can also be found on the following children's musical recordings:

- *All You Need Is Love: Beatles Songs for Kids.* Music for Little People, 1999.

- *One Light, One Sun* by Raffi. Troubadour, 1985.

⓪⓪⓪⓪⓪⓪⓪⓪⓪⓪⓪⓪⓪

Picture Book

No Ordinary Olive by Roberta Baker, illustrated by Debbie Tilley. Little, Brown, and Company, 2002. Olive Elizabeth Julia Jerome loves to be different from everybody else. This gets her in trouble with her principal. After painting a jungle scene on his desk without permission, she learns that it's okay to be expressive, but she needs to be more considerate of other people. The audience will laugh out loud when they first meet newborn Olive in the hospital's maternity ward hollering, "Hey, where does a baby get something to eat around here?"

Oscar's Half Birthday by Bob Graham. Candlewick Press, 2005. Baby Oscar's family celebrates his six-month birthday because "no one can wait for his whole birthday." They walk through the city to the top of Bellevue Hill. Several admiring city folk join in to sing "Happy Birthday" to Oscar. Have the audience join in with the song to simulate that "the whole hillside is singing."

Musical Activity

"One Finger, One Thumb"
Traditional

This is a staple in my story programs. It always remains fresh because of the flexibility of changing the verses. Instruct the children to hold up one finger and one thumb and move them. I ask the kids halfway through the activity if they're too tired to continue. They always respond back with a loud "No!"

> One finger, one thumb, keep moving.
> One finger, one thumb, keep moving.
> One finger, one thumb, keep moving
> And we'll all be happy today.
>
> *(Add body parts to subsequent verses.)*
>
> 2. One finger, one thumb, one elbow, keep moving …
>
> 3. One finger, one thumb, one elbow, two feet, keep moving …
>
> 4. One finger, one thumb, one elbow, two feet, one head, keep moving …
>
> 5. One finger, one thumb, one elbow, two feet, one head, one (*make a raspberry noise*), keep moving …
>
> 6. One finger, one thumb, one elbow, two feet, one head, one (*raspberry*), one tongue, keep moving …
>
> 7. One finger, one thumb, one elbow, two feet, one head, one (*raspberry*), one tongue, stand up sit down, keep moving …

Finish your last line by stating in an exhausted voice, "And we'll all be tired today!"

You can chant the lines or learn the melody from the following recording: *Wee Sing Children's Songs and Fingerplays* (Price, Stern, Sloan, 1979).

Picture Book

Olivia Saves the Circus by Ian Falconer. Atheneum, 2001. The first children's book character I thought of for this "O" theme was that great Falconer creation—Olivia the pig. Olivia returns to school after summer vacation and tells her class a whopper to end all whoppers. Apparently, Olivia went to the circus only to find that "all the circus people were out with ear infections." Luckily, Olivia knew how to do everything. She drew pictures on herself with a marker to take over for the Tattooed Lady. She also tamed the lion, juggled, rode the unicycle, walked on the high wire, and flew on the trapeze. She ends her story with a quickly added, "Then one time my dad took me sailing The End" (with "The End" appearing in tiny font). The look on her teacher's face is priceless.

ⓞⓞⓞⓞⓞⓞⓞⓞⓞⓞ

Movement Activity

"Oliver Twist, Can You Do This?"
Traditional

This is a different Oliver Twist activity from the one listed on page 31. Have the children stand and follow this ditty.

> Oliver Twist, can you do this?
>
> If so, do so.
>
> •   Number one … touch your tongue.
>
> •   Number two … touch your shoe.
>
> •   Number three … touch your knee.
>
> •   Number four … touch the floor.
>
> •   Number five … jump so high.

Picture Book

Daddy All Day Long by Francesca Rusackas, illustrated by Priscilla Burris. HarperCollins, 2004. Owen the pig and his father tell each other they love each other more than chocolate milk, more than two pancakes "with bananas on top," more than three piggyback rides, and so on up through one hundred fireflies, one thousand stars in the sky, and "one million zillion kisses!" Ask the kids in the audience if they can add to this list. I had a boy blurt out, "A ba-thrillion universes!" (Or something like that.)

◎◎◎◎◎◎◎◎◎◎◎◎◎

Poem

Oh, No! Where are My Pants? And Other Disasters: Poems edited by Lee Bennett Hopkins, illustrated by Wolf Erlbruch. HarperCollins, 2005. This collection of poems contains 14 worrisome poems—some humorous, some serious—by several different poets. Pick and choose any appropriate poems. Favorites include "Nightmare," by Judith Viorst, in which the title character is dressed in his best purple shirt, buckskin vest, cowboy boots, but—Oh, No!—no pants. Another humorous poem is "A Million Miles from Tallahassee," by Alice Schertle, in which a student blurts out that the capital of Florida is "Tassaloma" and is razzed by his classmates.

Picture Book

Old MacDonald Had a Woodshop by Lisa Shulman, illustrated by Ashley Wolff. Putnam, 2002. Old MacDonald is portrayed as a female sheep. She has a saw that goes "zztt zztt here and a zztt zztt there, here a zztt, there a zztt, everywhere a zztt zztt." Not only will the audience members enjoy making the noises, but they will also be able to add accompanying actions. Old MacDonald also has a drill ("rurr rurr"), a hammer ("tap tap"), a chisel ("chip chip"), a file ("scritch scratch"), a screwdriver ("squeak squeak"), and a paintbrush ("swish swash"). By the end of the book, Old MacDonald and her barnyard friends have made a model of the farm.

◎◎◎◎◎◎◎◎◎◎◎◎◎

Musical Activity

"Old MacDonald Had an Owl"
Traditional; new words by Rob Reid.

I had fun thinking of items that began with "O" that Old MacDonald might have had on his or her farm.

> Old MacDonald had a farm,
> E-I-E-I-O.
> And on this farm he had an Owl!
> E-I-E-I-O.
>
> With a "Whoo Whoo" here,
> And a "Whoo Whoo" there,
> Here a "Whoo," there a "Whoo,"
> Everywhere a "Whoo Whoo."
> Old MacDonald had a farm, E-I-E-I-O.
>
> Old MacDonald had a farm,
> E-I-E-I-O.
> And on this farm he had an Ogre!
> E-I-E-I-O.

With an "Aargh Aargh" here,
And an "Aargh Aargh" there,
Here an "Aargh," there an "Aargh,"
Everywhere an "Aargh Aargh."

A "Whoo Whoo" here,
And a "Whoo Whoo" there,
Here a "Whoo," there a "Whoo,"
Everywhere a "Whoo Whoo."
Old MacDonald had a farm, E-I-E-I-O.

Old MacDonald had a farm,
E-I-E-I-O.
And on his farm he had an Octopus!
E-I-E-I-O.

With a "Hug Hug" here,
And a "Hug Hug" there,
Here a "Hug," there a "Hug,"
Everywhere a "Hug Hug."

An "Aargh Aargh" here
And an "Aargh Aargh" there,
Here an "Aargh," there an "Aargh,"
Everywhere an "Aargh Aargh."

A "Whoo Whoo" here
And a "Whoo Whoo" there,
Here a "Whoo," there a "Whoo,"
Everywhere a "Whoo Whoo."
Old MacDonald had a farm, E-I-E-I-O.

Old MacDonald had a farm,
E-I-E-I-O.
And on his farm he had an Onion!
E-I-E-I-O.

With a "Waah Waah" here,
And a "Waah Waah" there,
Here a "Waah," there a "Waah,"
Everywhere a "Waah Waah."

A "Hug Hug" here,
And a "Hug Hug" there,
Here a "Hug," there a "Hug,"
Everywhere a "Hug Hug."

An "Aargh Aargh" here,
And an "Aargh Aargh" there,
Here an "Aargh," there an "Aargh,"
Everywhere an "Aargh Aargh."

A "Whoo Whoo" here,
And a "Whoo Whoo" there,
Here a "Whoo," there a "Whoo,"
Everywhere a "Whoo Whoo."
Old MacDonald had a farm, E-I-E-I-O.

Finish the program by serving "O" shaped treats such as Fruit Loops or Cheerios bars; and/or treats that begin with the letter "O," such as orange slices or oatmeal bars.

Ⓞ Ⓞ Ⓞ Ⓞ Ⓞ Ⓞ Ⓞ Ⓞ Ⓞ Ⓞ

Backup Picture Books

Bedhead by Margie Palatini, illustrated by Jack E. Davis. Simon & Schuster, 2000. Oliver wakes up to find his hair is out of control. His family tries to comb it, but it boings into a big clump "that looked just like a cat's coughed-up fur ball." They try spraying, putting in mousse, and brushing his hair before placing a hat on Oliver's head to cover it. The trouble is, when Oliver arrives at school, he finds out that it's picture day. The book has a long text to read, but there are fun sound effects, especially on the occasional "B-B-B-Boing!"

Grandpa's Overalls by Tony Crunk, illustrated by Scott Nash. Orchard Books, 2001. Grandpa's blue work overalls run away, leaving Grandpa flustered. "… A man can't work in nothin' but his long-handled drawers." Soon, the whole family and several neighbors are chasing the runaway overalls. The neighbors wind up pitching in with the chores, thus giving Grandpa an unexpected day off. "I peeked in on him once, and he didn't seem to mind it too bad." The overalls are eventually spotted dancing with Grandma's nightgown. "Gracious me …

A body can't sleep without her long-tailed nightie. After 'em!" And the chase begins again.

Joseph Had a Little Overcoat by Simms Taback. Viking, 1999. Taback's Caldecott Award winning picture book is based on a traditional Yiddish folksong (the musical score is included in the book's back matter for the musically-inclined storyteller). The die-cut holes on the pages emphasize the overcoat getting smaller over the years and turning into a jacket, a vest, a scarf, a necktie, a handkerchief, a button, and eventually, the story that led to this book.

Oliver Finds His Way by Phyllis Root, illustrated by Christopher Denise. Candlewick Press, 2002. Oliver is a small anthropomorphic bear cub who wanders away from his country home into the woods. He worries that he won't be able to find his way back to his parents. He hits upon the idea to roar. Have the audience roar along with Oliver to attract the attention of Oliver's parents.

Ollie by Olivier Dunrea. Houghton Mifflin, 2003. We are introduced to Ollie the gosling while he's still in his egg. Gossie and Gertie have been waiting for weeks for Ollie to hatch. Ollie refuses to come out of the egg and rolls along on a little journey before hatching on the last page. A companion book that features Ollie is *Ollie the Stomper* (Houghton Mifflin, 2003).

Otto Goes to School by Todd Parr. Little, Brown, and Company, 2005. Otto the dog is excited about going to school. He learns vital things, such as how to wag his tail without knocking things over; that shoes are for wearing, not eating; don't pull the cat's tail; and take turns going to the bathroom (Parr's illustration shows dogs lined up to use a tree). Other Otto books in the series include:

- *Otto Goes to Bed.* Little, Brown, and Company, 2003.
- *Otto Goes to Camp.* Little, Brown, and Company, 2004.
- *Otto Goes to the Beach.* Little, Brown, and Company, 2003.
- *Otto Goes to School.* Little, Brown, and Company, 2005.
- *Otto Has a Birthday Party.* Little, Brown, and Company, 2004.

Old (And Not So Old) Favorites

The Missing Piece Meets the Big O by Shel Silverstein. HarperCollins, 1981.

Officer Buckle and Gloria by Peggy Rathmann. Putnam, 1995.

Old Black Fly by Jim Aylesworth, illustrated by Stephen Gammell. Henry Holt & Company, 1992.

Oliver by Syd Hoff. HarperCollins, 1960.

Owen by Kevin Henkes. Greenwillow Books, 1993.

Owl Babies by Martin Waddell, illustrated by Patrick Benson. Candlewick Press, 1992.

Owl Moon by Jane Yolen, illustrated by John Schoenherr. Philomel, 1987.

A Last Word on the "Oh, No" Theme

Here are some more "O" words and names to consider. You may find some books featuring them to your liking.

Opossum	Olympics	Opera
Orchestra	Oak	Ocelot
Opal	Operation	Operator
Orangutan	Orbit	Origami
Orphans	Ostriches	Otters
Outdoors	Outlaws	Oxen
Ocean	Oscar	

And consider featuring the works of the following children's picture book author/illustrators regardless if the particular book features "O" objects or characters.

- Kevin O'Malley

- Jan Ormerod

- Helen Oxenbury

Oh, the Weather Outside Is Frightful

Stories and activities about snow days and frightful winter weather are perfect for a story program, whether you conduct it in Barrow, Alaska, or Key West, Florida, or points in between. As the children enter the program area, play a recording of the popular song "Let It Snow," which contains the theme's title phrase and can be found on countless Christmas recordings. Greet the children wearing a large winter hat, oversized mittens, and an extra-long scarf. Feel free to shed these garments once the program begins, lest you faint in front of your audience. Ask the kids to imagine that it is very cold outside. Brrr! Lead them in a round of shivering and teeth-chattering demonstrations. Ask them to make the sound of the cold, north wind. Tell them that no matter how cold it might be outdoors, they're in for some warm, comforting stories inside.

Picture Book

Straight to the Pole by Kevin O'Malley. Walker & Co., 2003. This is a fun short book to read to open the program. We see a lone hiker struggling over "hills and mountains" through a heavy snowstorm. He is about to give up when he sees a "wolf" approaching (a friendly dog). Soon, a rescue crew arrives (his friends carrying sleds). The journey to the pole is over! (The pole is actually the bus stop.) Read this fun text with an overly dramatic delivery.

Short Story/Demonstration

Here's a fun little comedic bit you can act out between picture books. Check out the one-page entry from *McBroom's Almanac* by Sid Fleischman (Little, Brown, and Company, 1984) titled "How to Keep Warm

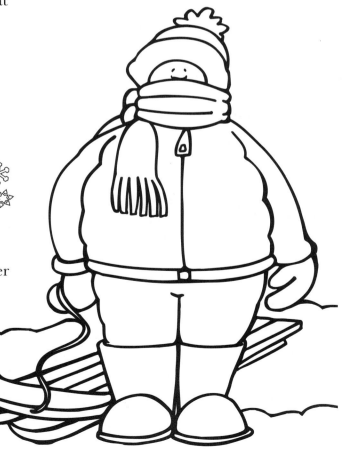

All Winter with One Stick of Wood." The basic premise of the joke is that you take one piece of wood and one piece of newspaper. Place the newspaper in your pocket. The instructions tell you to throw the stick with all of your might while facing due south. Run as fast as you can, pick up the stick and, once again, throw it. Continue doing so until you "reach a climate that calls for fanning yourself with the newspaper…" You can then throw the stick away. Have fun miming all of the actions while you teach the audience these wild instructions.

Picture Book

It Feels Like Snow by Nancy Cote. Boyds Mills Press, 2003. An older woman named Alice is able to predict snow when her big toe throbs, her nose tingles, and her elbows click. Her neighbors don't believe her predictions and are caught unprepared for a series of snowstorms, the last of which dumps snow waist-high. Alice helps her grateful neighbors who learn to heed Alice's built-in snow predictors.

Movement Activity

"The Bundle-Up Dance"
by Rob Reid

Have the children stand and dance in place to this little scat-like ditty. Have them repeat the second line of each verse with you.

Bundle-up, doot-doot-doodley-doot,
  Bundle-up, doot-doot-doodley-doot.

Snow pants, doot-doot-doodley-doot,
(Mime putting on snow pants.)
  Snow pants, doot-doot-doodley-doot.

Winter coat, doot-doot-doodley-doot,
(Mime putting on winter coat.)
  Winter coat, doot-doot-doodley-doot.

Two boots, doot-doot-doodley-doot,
(Mime putting on boots.)
  Two boots, doot-doot-doodley-doot.

Warm hat, doot-doot-doodley-doot,
(Mime putting on hat.)
  Warm hat, doot-doot-doodley-doot.

Long scarf, doot-doot-doodley-doot,
(Mime wrapping scarf around neck.)
  Long scarf, doot-doot-doodley-doot.

Two gloves, doot-doot-doodley-doot,
(Mime putting on gloves.)
  Two gloves, doot-doot-doodley-doot.

Let's play, doot-doot-doodley-doot,
(Dance in place.)
  In the snow, doot-doot-doodley-doot.

Bundle-up! Yeah!

Picture Book

This Place in the Snow by Rebecca Bond. Dutton Children's Books, 2004. The snow covers everything. The children wake up to the sound of a snowplow and rush outside. They decide to make an enormous "kingdom" out of the mound left by the plow. They make tunnels, snow floors, and snow spirals. The kids in the audience will be awestruck by the illustration of the final creation. Don't feel bad if your audience is anxious to leave the program to create their own snow kingdoms.

Musical Activity

Have everyone stand up and get their wiggles out with Greg and Steve's movement song titled "The Freeze" from their recordings *Kids in Motion* (Youngheart Records, 1987) or *We All Live Together, Vol. 2* (Youngheart Records, 1978). Simply play the recording, have the kids dance or move in any style, and when the music stops, everyone freezes in their position. "Now you can dance any way you please / But listen closely for The Freeze."

Picture Book

Axle Annie by Robin Pulver, illustrated by Tedd Arnold. Dial, 1999. The kids of Burskyville never have a snow day because of the heroics of school bus driver Axle Annie. Annie always makes it up Tiger Hill, the toughest hill in Burskyville, no matter how bad the weather conditions. Of course, not everyone is happy. Shifty Rhodes, the nastiest school bus driver in Burskyville, complains to the Grouch and Grump Club about not having a day off. Shifty enlists the aid of the new owner of the Burskyville ski resort who adds extra layers of snow to Tiger Hill. Axle Annie faces her toughest challenge yet.

Musical Activity

"The Wheels on Axle Annie's Bus"
Traditional; new words by Rob Reid, sung to the tune of "The Wheels on the Bus."

The wheels on Annie's bus go
Spinnety-spin,
Spinnety-spin, spinnety-spin.
(Make a whirling motion with your hands with an occasional "twisting out-of-control" flip of the hands.)
The wheels on Annie's bus go
Spinnety-spin,
All around the town.

The kids on Annie's bus go
Shivery-shake,
Shivery-shake, shivery-shake.
(Wrap your arms around yourself and shiver as if cold. Sing with chattering teeth.)
The kids on Annie's bus go
Shivery-shake,
All around the town.

The bus climbs Tiger Hill
Ever-so-slow,
Ever-so-slow, ever-so-slow.
(Hold hands on imaginary steering wheel and lean back as if climbing a hill.)
The bus climbs Tiger Hill
Ever-so-slow,
All around the town.

Everyone sings out
"Hey! We made it!
Hey! We made it, Hey! We made it!"
(Pump your fists in the air.)
Everyone sings out
"Hey! We made it!"
All around the town.

Picture Book

Totally Polar by Marty Crisp, illustrated by Viv Eisner. Rising Moon, 2001. This funny imagination story segues nicely into the final activity. Peter Petrosky MacGregor O'Toole worries that it will snow so much that his family won't be able to open their door, that he'll need a forklift to build the snowman's head, icebergs will form in the pond, and he'll have to burn his homework to keep the fireplace roaring. The book's joke is that it's June. Peter later goes to the beach wearing mukluks for beach shoes and wool long johns for swim trunks.

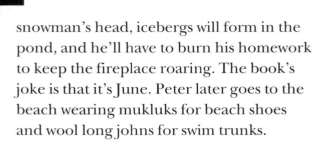

Musical Activity

Finish the program by putting on sunglasses, a Hawaiian shirt, and suntan lotion on your nose. Throw down a beach blanket or two and have everyone dance away the winter blues. Play a selection from the recording *Catch a Wave: Beach Songs for Kids* (Music for Little People, 2000). Titles include "Surfin' Safari," "Wipe Out," "Surfin's U.S.A.," and more.

Backup Picture Books

The Abominable Snow Teacher by Lisa Passen. Henry Holt & Company, 2004. Miss Irma Birmbaum has the reputation of being the "toughest teacher in town." When school is cancelled due to a snowstorm, Miss Irma Birmbaum tries her best to open up the school. She transforms into an Abominable Snow Teacher and unintentionally scares the children as they play in the snow. The wind picks up, spins Miss Irma Birmbaum around, and she starts playing in the snow like a little kid. This story is weird, but fun.

Avalanche by Michael J. Rosen, illustrated by David Butler. Candlewick Press, 1998. This tall tale relates how an avalanche began when Bobby tossed a snowball. It rolled down a hill and grew bigger and bigger, wiping out a whole alphabetical litany of items. The snowball even caused glaciers and iced the planet before launching into space, hitting stars and filling the universe before falling back to Earth. As the snowball rolls back, it gets smaller and smaller and is finally caught by the boy's dog Zippy. "Gadzooks! What a throw!"

Bearsie Bear and the Surprise Sleepover Party by Bernard Waber. Houghton Mifflin, 1997. One bitter cold night, Bearsie Bear finds himself host to Moosie Moose, Cowsie Cow, Piggie Pig, Foxie Fox, Goosie Goose, and Porkie Porcupine. This book is a delight to simply read and share the pictures or turn into a reader's theater presentation with the help of older kids. It's very simple to fashion your own script for a classroom or library program. In addition to the animal characters, split the narration among three readers. Assign Narrator 1 all of the "said" lines. Normally, when developing a reader's theater script from another text, you'll want to remove the various "he said" and "she said" lines. Here, however, they add to the lively, tongue-twisting humor. For example,

Moosie Moose: It's me, Moosie Moose.
Narrator 1: … said Moosie Moose.
Bearsie Bear: Moosie Moose?
Narrator 1: … said Bearsie Bear.
Moosie Moose: Yes, Moosie Moose.
Narrator 1: … said Moosie Moose.

Assign Narrator 2 the role of making the sound effects, such as the various wind noises and the animals knocking, tapping, and scratching at the door. Narrator 3 can read all of the other non-dialogue lines.

Best Little Wingman by Janet Allen, illustrated by Jim Postier. Boyds Mills Press, 2005. Janny goes for a night ride with her father, who drives the big snowplow. Her job is to "pull the lever that raised the plow's right wing, so the big plow didn't knock over people's mailboxes along their road." The two help a veterinarian get to a sick horse and they pull a stranded vehicle from a snow bank. When Janny falls asleep, her father drops her off at home before heading back out into the cold night.

Blizzard by Carole Gerber, illustrated by Marty Husted. Whispering Coyote, 2001. This short, quiet book contrasts the fierce, cold weather outside a boy's rural home with the warm and bright interior. While the snow piles up, the boy snuggles and drinks hot cocoa. When the wind dies down, the boy ventures outside to make a snow angel.

I'm Not Feeling Well Today by Shirley Neitzel, illustrated by Nancy Winslow Parker. Greenwillow Books, 2001. A young boy describes how he doesn't feel well in this cumulative verse designed in the style of "The House that Jack Built." Parker's illustrations interact with the text in the form of a rebus story, which may also lend itself to a felt board adaptation. The various pictures show a box of tissues, a blanket, a pillow, a cat, food, a television, and various toys. When the boy learns that school is closed due to bad weather, he suddenly feels "well today!"

Snow Day by Lynn Plourde, illustrated by Hideko Takahashi. Simon & Schuster, 2001. Kids wake up to a snow day and celebrate inside with an almost rap-like poetic text. "Wooooo-ooooo! / Wild, whirling wind / Crashes limbs to lines / Lights dance. / Flick-a-lick. / Lights die. Flick-a-flooooo." When the storm ends, the children play outside in the "snow day, noisy snow day" before retiring once more in the "snow day, sleepy snow day."

Old (And Not So Old) Favorites

The Big Snow by Berta Hader and Elmer Hader. Macmillan, 1948.

Birthday Blizzard by Bonnie Pryor, illustrated by Molly Delaney. William Morrow & Co., 1993.

The Blizzard by Betty Ren Wright, illustrated by Ron Himler. Holiday House, 2003.

Boo and Baa in Windy Weather by Olof Landström and Lena Landström. R & S Books, 1996.

Brave Irene by William Steig. Farrar, Straus, and Giroux, 1986.

Brrr! by James Stevenson. Greenwillow Books, 1991.

Edward's Overwhelming Overnight by Rosemary Wells. Dial, 1995.

Katy and the Big Snow by Virginia Lee Burton. Houghton Mifflin, 1943.

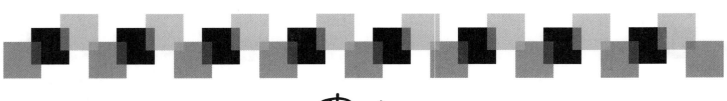

Pets

Advertise in advance and invite audience members to bring their favorite stuffed animals. Have a few stuffed animals and puppets on hand for those kids who didn't bring one from home. The animals can sit with the kids as their special guests. Before the first story begins, ask the kids to show off their pet friends. Ask them what other types of animals can be considered a pet by some people.

Picture Book

The Perfect Pet by Margie Palatini, illustrated by Bruce Whatley. HarperCollins, 2003. Elizabeth "really, really, really wanted a pet." Her parents, however, "really, really, really did not." They give Elizabeth a cactus instead. Elizabeth eventually makes a pet out of a bug. The text is long but flows at a nice clip due to Palatini's trademark humor and witty dialogue. The parents' reactions when Elizabeth springs a new idea past them are especially fun to read aloud:

"'Huh? What? Who?' said Father."
"'Who? What? Huh?' said Mother."

Picture Book

The Best Pet of All by David LaRochelle, illustrated by Hanako Wakiyama. Dutton Children's Book, 2004. I gave this picture book my coveted Robbie Award Honors for the funniest children's book of the year (a close second to Mo Willems's *Knuffle Bunny*). A boy asks his mother for a pet dog. When she refuses, he asks her for a pet dragon. Amused, she gives him permission. Unfortunately, the dragon has terrible manners and creates a mess in the house. The boy informs his mother that dragons don't like dogs. When a dog appears at the front door, the dragon leaves and the mother exclaims that dogs are indeed the best pets a family could own. See if your audience members catch the subtle high sign between the boy and the dragon at the end of the book.

Musical Activity

"Dogs and Cats and Guinea Pigs"
by Rob Reid. Sung to the tune of "Heads, Shoulders, Knees, and Toes."

Have the children make the following motions and sound effect for each animal:

- Dogs: *Pant with tongues out.*
- Cats: *Lick the back of their hand.*
- Guinea Pigs: *Blink as if just waking up and looking around (which is how I usually find guinea pigs).*
- Birds: *Flap arms as wings.*
- Fish: *Purse lips and hold hands behind ears as if they were gills.*
- Snakes: *Flick tongues in and out.*
- Mice: *Brush behind ears as if cleaning them with paws.*

> Dogs and cats and guinea pigs,
> Guinea pigs,
>
> Dogs and cats and guinea pigs,
> Guinea Pigs,
>
> Birds and fish and snakes and mice,
> Dogs and cats and guinea pigs,
> Guinea pigs.

Picture Book

That New Animal by Emily Jenkins, illustrated by Pierre Pratt. Farrar, Straus, and Giroux, 2005. The two dogs, FudgeFudge and Marshmallow, do not like the new animal in the house, which we see right away on the cover and the title page, is a new human baby. The people in the house ignore the two dogs, except when the dogs misbehave to get attention. However, when Grandpa arrives and tries to pick up the new animal, FudgeFudge and Marshmallow become very protective and chase Grandpa away. The two dogs slowly appreciate the new animal, especially when its first word is "Da," which certainly means "dog."

Musical Activity

"Rags"
Traditional

Have the children stand and move to the following popular camp song favorite.

> I have a dog, his name is Rags.
> *(Point to self.)*
>
> He eats so much his tummy sags.
> *(Point to stomach.)*
>
> His ears flip-flop,
> *(Shake a hand behind each ear.)*
> His tail wig-wags.
> *(Shake hips side to side.)*
>
> And when he walks,
> He walks zig-zag.
> *(Make diagonal slashes in front of your body with pointing fingers.)*

"Rags" aka "My Dog Rags" can be found on the following recordings:

- *Great Big Hits* by Sharon, Lois, and Bram. Elephant Records, 1992.
- *Nancy Cassidy's Kids Songs: The Sing-Along Songbook* (with CD) by Nancy Cassidy. Klutz, 2004.

Picture Books

Chewy Louie by Howie Schneider. Rising Moon, 2000. This wonderful tall tale shows a puppy literally eating the family out of house and home. Louie chews his bowl, the toys, a porch, lumber stacked on a lumber truck, the vet's office, the dog trainer's cane, a musician's guitar, and more. Louie finally outgrows his chewing phase. However, there's a surprise embedded in the endpapers that the kids in the audience are sure to notice.

Five Creatures by Emily Jenkins, illustrated by Tomasz Bogacki. Farrar, Straus, and Giroux, 2001. Emily Jenkins is back with another picture book featuring pets. This time we meet two cats and three humans. These five share several common traits (and differences, too). Let the kids in the audience tell you which of the five have orange hair, like to eat mice, don't like taking baths, can get up on a high stool, can crawl under the refrigerator, can climb trees, and more. The illustrations provide all the necessary answers in this highly interactive book.

Fingerplay

"The Puppy and the Cat"
Traditional

This one never fails to get the little ones to laugh.

> See the little puppy dog,
> *(Hold up one fist.)*
> See the little cat.
> *(Hold up other fist.)*
> Puppy goes to sleep just like that.
> *(Put head on hands, close eyes.)*

Kitty sneaks up quietly,
(Move the "cat" fist near the "dog" fist.)
Tickles puppy's chin.
(Tickle the "dog" fist with one finger.)
Puppy wakes up startled,
(Hold "dog" fist open, fingers outstretched.)
Let the chase begin!
(Have one fist chase the other all through the air.)

Picture Book

On the First Day of Grade School by Emily Brenner, illustrated by Bruce Whatley. HarperCollins, 2004. The text is based on the song "The Twelve Days of Christmas." A teacher gets the following "classroom pets" from her students: "On the first day of grade school / My students gave to me / A python that didn't squeeze me." The other verses include two buzzing bees, three fat rats, four burping goats, five snoring pigs, six screaming chickens, seven skating monkeys, eight sick gorillas, nine skunks a-stinkin', ten toads on tiptoe, eleven prancing ponies, and twelve smart zookeepers. The double-page spreads get more and more crowded. It's hard to read the text without launching into song (so go ahead).

Musical Activity

"I Had a (Pet) Rooster"
Traditional; new words and motions by Rob Reid.

Ask the kids one more time what types of animals can be considered pets. Sing the popular folk song "I Had a Rooster" with the following new verses with new movement activities and sound effects.

I had a rooster and my rooster pleased me.
I fed my rooster 'neath the old chestnut tree.
My little rooster went, "Cock-a-doodle-doo-dee-doodle-dee-doodle-dee-doodle-dee-doo."

I had a dog and my dog pleased me.
I fed my dog 'neath the old chestnut tree.
My little dog went, "Aa-rrr-ooooo!"
(Exaggerate a loud howl.)
My little rooster went, "Cock-a-doodle-doo-dee-doodle-dee-doodle-dee-doodle-dee-doo."

I had a cat and my cat pleased me.
I fed my cat 'neath the old chestnut tree.
My little cat went, "Spit! Hiss. Spit!"
(Make pawing motions.)
My little dog went, "Aa-rrr-ooooo!"
My little rooster went, "Cock-a-doodle-doo-dee-doodle-dee-doodle-dee-doodle-dee-doo."

I had a goldfish and my goldfish pleased me.
I fed my goldfish 'neath the old chestnut tree.
My little goldfish went, "Blub, blub, blub."
(Put hands behind ears and wave as gills.)
My little cat went, "Spit! Hiss! Spit!"
My little dog went, "Aa-rrr-ooooo!"
My little rooster went, "Cock-a-doodle-doo-dee-doodle-dee-doodle-dee-doodle-dee-doo."

I had a lizard and my lizard pleased me.
I fed my lizard 'neath the old chestnut tree.
My little lizard went,
(Move tongue in and out without a sound.)
My little goldfish went, "Blub, blub, blub."
My little cat went, "Spit! Hiss! Spit!"
My little dog went, "Aa-rrr-ooooo!"
My little rooster went, "Cock-a-doodle-doo-dee-doodle-dee-doodle-dee-doodle-dee-doo."

I had a hamster and my hamster pleased me.
I fed my hamster 'neath the old chestnut tree.
My little hamster went, "Squeak, squeak."
(Make paddle motions as if running on a squeaky wheel.)
My little lizard went, *(Move tongue.)*
My little goldfish went, "Blub, blub, blub."
My little cat went, "Spit! Hiss! Spit!"
My little dog went, "Aa-rrr-ooooo!"
My little rooster went, "Cock-a-doodle-doo-dee-doodle-dee-doodle-dee-doodle-dee-doo."

I had a rabbit and my rabbit pleased me.
I fed my rabbit 'neath the old chestnut tree.
My little rabbit went,
(Wiggle nose without making a sound.)
My little hamster went, "Squeak, squeak."
My little lizard went, *(Move tongue.)*
My little goldfish went, "Blub, blub, blub."
My little cat went, "Spit! Hiss! Spit!"
My little dog went, "Aa-rrr-ooooo!"
My little rooster went, "Cock-a-doodle-doo-dee-doodle-dee-doodle-dee-doodle-dee-doo."

I had a parrot and my parrot pleased me.
I fed my parrot 'neath the old chestnut tree.
My little parrot went, "Squawk! This song is done! Squawk!"

"I Had a Rooster" can be found on *Singin' in the Bathtub* by John Lithgow (Sony, 1999).

Backup Picture Books

The Birthday Fish by Dan Yaccarino. Henry Holt & Company, 2005. Cynthia is disappointed when she receives a goldfish for her birthday instead of a pony. When she starts to drop the goldfish down the drain, the goldfish speaks up and asks Cynthia to set it free in a nearby lake. Cynthia places the goldfish bowl on a stroller and they take off through town. The two bond along the way, which leads to a satisfying conclusion.

I Wanna Iguana by Karen Kaufman Orloff, illustrated by David Catrow. Putnam, 2004. A young boy tries to convince his mother to allow him to adopt "Mikey Gulligan's baby iguana." For every reason the boy gives for owning the iguana, his mother counters with a valid point why it would not be a good idea. The boy and his mother communicate via letters. This makes a great presentation for two voices—snare a co-worker or volunteer to read the dialogue with you.

My Big Dog by Janet Stevens and Susan Stevens Crummel. Golden Books, 1999. Despite the title and cover shot of a golden retriever, this picture book is actually more about the house's pet cat, Merl. Merl is upset when the new dog arrives and runs away. Eventually, the dog finds Merl and brings him back home. Merl decides that the dog missed him.

Not Norman: A Goldfish Story by Kelly Bennett, illustrated by Noah Z. Jones. Candlewick Press, 2005. At first, the young narrator finds his pet fish to be too boring. "All Norman does is swim around and around and around and around and around and around and around …" The boy considers taking Norman back to the pet store. However, in the middle of the night, the youngster hears scary noises. He notices that Norman is wide awake and is comforted by that fact.

So, What's It Like to Be a Cat? by Karla Kuskin, illustrated by Betsy Lewin. Atheneum, 2005. A young boy decides to interview his cat. The cat describes his many habits and moods. Among the boy's questions are "Do you have a kitty bed?" and "Do you roar?" The boy's final two questions concern the people who live with the cat. The cat replies that although he wishes the humans well, "I'd rather be a cat."

The Very Kind Rich Lady and Her One Hundred Dogs by Chinlun Lee. Candlewick Press, 2001. Get ready to read one hundred dog names, not once, but twice! We start by meeting a dog whose name is Papa and work our way through Bingo, "who was always late." Other names include Groucho, Harpo, Chico, and Mrs. Fifi and her pups Eeny, Meeny, Miney, and Mo. Every day, the very kind rich lady brushes each dog "at least ten strokes each," searches their coats for fleas, feeds them on one hundred plates, fusses over them, talks to them, and calls them by name; hence the second run-through with the names— purely optional!

Old (And Not So Old) Favorites

Arthur's Pet Business by Marc Brown. Joy Street, 1990.

A Fish Out of Water by Helen Palmer, illustrated by P. D. Eastman. Random House, 1961.

Martha Speaks by Susan Meddaugh. Houghton Mifflin, 1992.

Mr. Putter and Tabby Walk the Dog by Cynthia Rylant, illustrated by Arthur Howard. Harcourt, 1994.

Three Stories You Can Read to Your Cat by Sara Swan Miller, illustrated by True Kelley. Houghton Mifflin, 1997.

Three Stories You Can Read to Your Dog by Sara Swan Miller, illustrated by True Kelley. Houghton Mifflin, 1995.

Walter's Tail by Lisa Campbell Ernst. Bradbury, 1992.

Royalty

This theme features kings and queens, princes and princesses, castles, knights, wizards, and dragons. Greet the children "royally" as they enter the program area. Bow deeply when they arrive. Play fanfare music, such as Aaron Copeland's "Fanfare for the Common Man" or a Bach adagio on the CD player. Wear a jester's hat and hand them a paper crown. Address them as "M'Lord" and "M'Lady" and beg they get comfortable for the "day's entertainment."

Picture Book

Good Night, Good Knight by Shelley Moore Thomas, illustrated by Jennifer Plecas. Dutton Children's Books, 2000. The Good Knight books by Thomas are two of my all-time favorite easy readers. In this first book, the Good Knight hears "a very large, very loud roar." Have the kids in the audience make a loud roar. The knight climbs on his horse and shouts "Away!" They "Clippety-Clop, Clippety-Clop" and find a cave with three tiny dragons. Have the kids slap their legs every time "Clippety-Clop" appears in the book. The knight makes several trips from the castle to the cave and back again—all to settle down the three dragons (in their jammies) for bed.

Chapter Book Selection

Knights of the Kitchen Table by Jon Scieszka. Viking, 1991. I've read the third chapter of this book to so many groups of children, that I almost have it memorized. This fun read finds the Time Warp Trio stranded back in medieval times and the infamous Black Knight thundering down on them. The boys find a way to outwit the villain and knock him out, only to come under attack from another threat. Kids of all ages will sit still to listen to this short chapter book selection with its combination of humor and adventure.

Movement Activity

"The Grand Old Duke of York"
Traditional

Have the kids follow the directions given in this old Mother Goose rhyme. Repeat it a second time going slightly faster.

> The Grand Old Duke of York,
> He had ten thousand men.
> He marched them up a hill,
> *(Everyone stands.)*
> He marched them down again.
> *(Everyone sits.)*
>
> And when they're up, they're up,
> *(Everyone stands.)*
> And when they're down, they're down.
> *(Everyone sits.)*
> But when they're only halfway up,
> *(Everyone crouches.)*
> They're neither up,
> *(Everyone stands straight.)*
> Nor down. *(Everyone sits.)*

Picture Books

Kitty Princess and the Newspaper Dress by Emma Carlow, illustrated by Trevor Dickinson. Candlewick Press, 2003. Kitty Princess is rude and bossy. She orders her Fairy Godmouse to make the best dress in the world for an upcoming ball. Kitty Princess is not satisfied with the results and decides to shop for her own outfit. Since she has never gone shopping by herself before, she makes many mistakes. She's also very rude the entire time. Kitty Princess orders shoes from a food store and winds up with watermelon shoes. She orders jewelry from a café and winds up with an edible necklace. She orders a dress from the newsstand and winds up with a newspaper dress. She finally realizes her behavior is wrong and she apologizes to everyone.

Who Wants a Dragon? by James Mayhew, illustrated by Lindsey Gardiner. Orchard Books, 2004. Nobody wants to hang around a baby dragon. The dragon is too big for the witch's broom. The knight is afraid of being bitten. The princess finds the dragon too muddy. The king and queen are simply too frightened and hide behind their thrones. In the end, the young dragon finds that his mommy wants him.

Movement Activity

"I'm a Mean Old Dragon"
Traditional

"I'm a Mean Old Dinosaur" was the name of this ditty when I first learned it. I simply changed one word.

> I'm a mean old dragon, *(Make a mean face.)*
> Big and tall. *(Hold hands overhead.)*
> Here is my tail, *(Hold hand behind you and swish it back and forth.)*
> Here is my claw. *(Make claws with hands.)*
>
> When I get hungry, *(Rub tummy.)*
> I just growl. *(Growl.)*
> Look out, everybody!
> I'm on the prowl!
> *(Make mean face again and hold up claws.)*

Picture Book

Serious Trouble by Arthur Howard. Harcourt, 2003. Prince Ernest doesn't want to be a king like his father. Being a king is much too serious. Ernest would rather be a jester. When Ernest finds himself face-to-face with a "fire-breathing, people-eating, three-headed dragon," he uses his wits to keep the dragon from eating him. The dragon promises to stop eating people if Ernest can make the dragon (all three heads) laugh. Ernest fails at making funny faces and tumbling, but scores when he tickles the dragon's feet.

Movement Activity

"Ar-Roo-Sta-Sha"
Traditional

Tell your audience that this would have been a good humorous activity for Ernest to use on the dragons in the previous picture book. They can learn it in case they ever need to make a dragon laugh. Ask everyone to stand and follow the directions (add each step to subsequent moves).

Chorus:

Ar-roo-sta-sha, Ar-roo-sta-sha,
 Ar-roo-sta-sha-sha, *(Dance in place.)*
Ar-roo-sta-sha, Ar-roo-sta-sha,
 Ar-roo-sta-sha-sha.

Thumbs up! *(Audience repeats "Thumbs up!"—and subsequent oral commands—and holds up thumbs.)*

(Chorus)

Thumbs up! Elbows back!
(Hold elbows back.)

(Chorus)

Thumbs up! Elbows back! Knees bent! *(Bend knees.)*

(Chorus)

Thumbs up! Elbows back! Knees bent! Knees together! *(Place knees together.)*

(Chorus)

Thumbs up! Elbows back! Knees bent! Knees together! Tongue out!
(Stick out tongue.)

(Chorus)

Thumbs up! Elbows back! Knees bent! Knees together! Tongue out! Turn around.
(Slowly spin in place.)

(Chorus)

Versions of this activity can be found as "Tooty Ta" or "A Tooty Ta" on the following children's recordings:

- *Dance Like This* by Mr. Al. Mr. Al, 2000.

- *Dr. Jean and Friends* by Jean Feldman. Progressive Music, 1998.

Backup Picture Books

An African Princess by Lyra Edmonds, illustrated by Anne Wilson. Candlewick Press, 2004. Lyra learns that she is from a long line of African princesses. Her schoolmates don't believe her. Lyra travels to Africa with her family to meet a real African princess, her Taunte May. When she arrives, Lyra is surprised to learn that Taunte May lives in a little brown house on stilts instead of a palace. Taunte May convinces Lyra to "remember to be proud of who you are."

Do Princesses Wear Hiking Boots? by Carmela LaVigna Coyle, illustrated by Mike and Carl Gordon. Rising Moon, 2003. A modern-day girl asks her mother a series of questions concerning princesses. Do they ride tricycles, climb trees, walk in the park, play in the sand and dirt, follow rules, cry and fuss, and snore? In the end, she wonders "do princesses seem at all like me?" Her mommy replies, "Look inside yourself and see …" A mirror is attached to the final page.

Get Well, Good Knight by Shelley Moore Thomas, illustrated by Jennifer Plecas. Dutton Children's Books, 2002. While the knight is out riding, he hears a noise. "Methinks I hear a sneeze." He and his horse "Clippety-Clop" to the cave to find the three dragons with "their heads hot with fever." The dragons sniffle, cough, and go "achoo!" They do this three times in the story. Cue your audience to make the sounds of the dragons. In order to help the young dragons, the knight asks a wizard to make some scaly-snail-y soup. The dragons turn up their noses. Next, the wizard makes some slimy-grimy soup. They once more turn up their noses. Finally, the knight's mother makes a batch of delicious chicken soup, which helps cure the dragons.

Little Ones Do! by Jana Novotny Hunter, illustrated by Sally Anne Lambert. Dutton Children's Books, 2001. A young dragon does a lot of daily activities that children in the audience will recognize. The dragon wakes up his parents in the morning, dawdles after breakfast, goes to school, looks at books, plays pony on Daddy's back, and finally, snuggles back in bed at the end of the day.

The Princesses Have a Ball by Teresa Bateman, illustrated by Lynne Cravath. Albert Whitman & Co., 2002. This is a

modern-day variation of the traditional fairy tale "The Twelve Dancing Princesses." The king tries to learn why his daughters are exhausted in the morning and wearing worn shoes. A cobbler named Jack learns that the princesses are going to a ball; not a dancing ball, however. They are playing basketball! Jack eventually designs athletic footwear for them and they invite their father, the king, to be the referee.

Princess Penelope by Todd Mack, illustrated by Julia Gran. Scholastic, 2003. Penelope is absolutely certain that she is a princess. She reads a lot of fairy tales, wears a crown, has chambermaids (stuffed animals), sits on thrones (including a car seat and a potty chair), has servants wait on her (Mom and Dad), and rides in a chariot (a stroller). Illustrator Gran reveals both the real world and the world of royalty as seen through Penelope's eyes.

The Seven Chinese Sisters by Kathy Tucker, illustrated by Grace Lin. Albert Whitman, 2003. Although there's no royalty in this story, it does feature a dragon that kidnaps the youngest of seven sisters. Each sister has a special talent and they combine their skills to rescue their sister. At the end, the younger sister's special talent is revealed. She's a storyteller "and she always told this story first."

The Sorcerer's Apprentice by Sally Grindley, illustrated by Thomas Taylor. Phyllis Fogelman Books, 2002. This is a nice version of the traditional story designed for younger audiences. The apprentice casts a spell to make the broomstick carry water from the well to fill the cauldron. The apprentice forgets the words to make the broomstick stop and soon the room is filled with water. The sorcerer returns to put a halt to the spell. He's angry at first but soon decides to give the apprentice a second chance.

Old (And Not So Old) Favorites

Cinderella Penguin, or, the Little Glass Flipper by Janet Perlman. Viking, 1992.

The 500 Hats of Bartholomew Cubbins by Dr. Seuss. Random House, 1938.

The Frog Prince—Continued by Jon Scieszka, illustrated by Steve Johnson. Viking, 1991.

The King's Stilts by Dr. Seuss. Random House, 1939.

Lazy Jack by Tony Ross. Dial, 1985.

The Paper Bag Princess by Robert Munsch, illustrated by Michael Martchenko. Annick Press, 1980.

The Princess and the Pea by Janet Stevens. Holiday House, 1982.

Rumpelstiltskin by Paul Galdone. Clarion Books, 1985.

Slow and Fast

This program features both speedy and very slow characters. Play one of the two following recordings as audience members enter the program area:

- "Quiet Moments" from *Quiet Moments with Greg and Steve* by Greg and Steve. Youngheart Records, 1983.

- "Slow Day" from *Bananaphone* by Raffi. MCA, 1994.

This program is designed to start off slowly, speed up in the middle, and then slow down again at the end. Start by asking the children if they can name some types of animals or objects that move very, very quickly. Next, ask if they can name some that move very, very slowly.

Picture Book

Slowly, Slowly, Slowly, Said the Sloth by Eric Carle. Philomel, 2002. Several jungle animals ask the sloth why it is so slow, quiet, boring, and lazy. After thinking about it for "a long, long, long time," sloth slowly responds with an incredible array of self-descriptive adjectives, such as "languid, stoic, impassive, sluggish, lethargic …" and concludes, "That's just how I am. I like to do things slowly, slowly, slowly."

Fingerplay

"Slowly, Slowly"
Traditional

Slowly, slowly, very slowly,
Creeps the garden snail.
("Walk" two fingers slowly up one arm.)

Slowly, slowly, very slowly,
Up the wooden rail.

Quickly, quickly, very quickly,
Runs the little mouse.
("Run" two fingers up and down one arm.)
Quickly, quickly, very quickly,

Round about the house.
("Run" the fingers around your body.)

Picture Book

Hi, Harry! by Martin Waddell, illustrated by Barbara Firth. Candlewick Press, 2003. This picture book has a very descriptive subtitle: "The Moving Story of How One Slow Tortoise Slowly Made a Friend."

Harry the tortoise tries in vain to make friends with the faster animals. He finally finds the perfect friend in Sam Snail. They play Slow Races, Heads In and Heads Out, and Turn Around and Turn Around Again. Have the audience members imitate Harry and Sam playing their slow games.

Activity

"Tongue Twisters"

Choose a very short tongue twister and have the children repeat it slowly after you, word for word. Repeat the process a few more times, each time speaking faster and faster. The last speedy recitation usually ends up with multiple slips of the tongues and lots of laughs. The following is good resource to use with a young crowd:

- *Busy Buzzing Bumblebees and Other Tongue Twisters* by Alvin Schwartz, illustrated by Paul Meisel. HarperCollins, 1982/rev. ed. 1992.

Some favorite tongue-twisting phrases from this book include:

- "Six sticky sucker sticks."
- "Sixty-six sneaky snakes."
- "Nellie Needle nibbles noodles."
- "Cheap sheep soup."

Picture Book

Roller Coaster by Marla Frazee. Harcourt, 2003. Frazee does a great job of capturing the anticipation and anxiety of a young girl as she waits for a ride on a roller coaster.

Once buckled in, the girl and her fellow passengers take the slow ascent to the top of the ride before whooshing, zipping, zooming, dipping, and diving around the track. One double-page spread shows the roller coaster doing a loop-de-loop; the reader must turn the book around and around to follow the text. Have fun with the vocal inflections as the ride speeds up. Subtle illustrations will alert the kids in the audience that the little girl is ready for another ride while the two biggest men from the roller coaster are very queasy.

Musical Activity

"Flight of the Bumblebee"
by Nikolay Rimsky-Korsakov

Have the children rise, stretch, and shake their hands to one of the fastest classical pieces. This famous composition can be found on several adult classical music records and the following children's recordings:

- *Baby Einstein: Playtime Music Box*. Buena Vista, 2004.
- *Elmo and the Orchestra*. Sony, 2001.

Picture Book

The Wheels on the Race Car by Alexander Zane, illustrated by James Warhola. Orchard Books, 2005. I've been doing my own variation of "The Wheels on the Bus," featuring a sports car, a rocket ship, and a donkey cart, for years. You can find the words and motions to my "New Wheels on the Bus" in my book *Family Storytime* (ALA, 1999). Zane focuses his variation of the popular children's song on a car race and everything and everyone involved with the race. The cry "Racers … Start your engines!!!" sets off an anthropomorphic group of drivers around the track. The racers and announcers yell "GO-GO-GO" as well as "SPEEDS ON BACK," "MAKES HIS MOVE," and "ZOOMS TO THE LEAD." Their cars go "ZIP-ZIP-ZIP," the gas from the gas can goes "GLUG-GLUG-GLUG," the mechanics go "ZIZZ-ZIZZ-ZIZZ," and the checkered flag goes "SWISH-SWISH-SWISH." The book's endpapers give visual clues so that the audience members can add movements to the various sound effects.

Musical Activity

"The Fast Food Song"
Traditional; sung to the tune of "Ram Sam Sam."

This movement song has been making the rounds at various summer camps and day cares. Have the children stand and act out this musical ode to modern day fast-food restaurants.

Motions:

Pizza Hut: *Make a triangle shape with your arms over your head.*

Kentucky Fried Chicken: *Flap your elbows up and down.*

McDonald's: *Put hands overhead in an arch shape.*

> A Pizza Hut, a Pizza Hut,
> Kentucky Fried Chicken and a Pizza Hut.
> A Pizza Hut, A Pizza Hut,

Kentucky Fried Chicken and a Pizza Hut.
McDonald's, McDonald's,
Kentucky Fried Chicken and a Pizza Hut.

I usually just do the above verse for the preschool crowd, but here are a few more variations that may also be a hit with certain audiences:

Motions:

Burger King: *Put hands on head with fingers in the air for a crown.*

Long John Silvers: *Mimic swishing a sword.*

Red Lobster: *Hold up both hands and move thumbs to simulate lobster claws.*

> A Burger King, a Burger King,
> Long John Silvers and a Burger King.
> A Burger King, a Burger King
> Long John Silvers and a Burger King.
> Red Lobster, Red Lobster,
> Long John Silvers and a Burger King.

Motions:

Dairy Queen: *Mime milking a cow.*

Chucky Cheese: *Mime throwing a pizza in the air.*

Roy Rogers: *Mime riding a horse.*

> A Dairy Queen, a Dairy Queen,
> Chucky Cheese and a Dairy Queen.
> A Dairy Queen, a Dairy Queen,
> Chucky Cheese and a Dairy Queen.
> Roy Rogers, Roy Rogers,
> Chucky Cheese and a Dairy Queen.

The melody to "Ram Sam Sam" can by found on the following children's musical recordings:

- *150 Fun Songs for Kids* by The Countdown Kids. Madacy, 2004.

- *Wigglin' Collection* by The Wiggles. Wiggles N' Tunes, 2002.

Picture Book

Snail City by Jane O'Connor, illustrated by Rick Brown. Grosset and Dunlap, 2001. Bring the program back down to a slow pace with the reading of this short picture book. All of the residents in Snail City like the Slow Life. There are no fast food restaurants, no fast lanes in the highway, and it takes forever to get their snail mail. However, one snail named Gail likes to go fast. She finishes first in every race (even though, in Snail City, "the last one is the winner"). The other kids make fun of her by calling her "Fastpoke." In the end, she uses her speed to save a baby snail from drowning.

Musical Activity

"Row, Row, Row Your Boat"
Traditional

Have the children exit the program area by miming the slow rowing of oars on a rowboat to this lazy tune. That means they will be exiting walking backwards, so emphasize that their movements should be very slow. As soon as they reach the door or open area, they should turn around and face front to greet their family or caregivers. This traditional tune can be found on the following recordings:

* *Country Tot.* Kidzup Productions, 1997.

* *Disney's Children's Favorites 1.* Disney, 1979.

* *101 Toddler Favorites.* Music for Little People, 2003.

* *Preschool Favorites.* Music for Little People, 2001.

Backup Picture Books

Come Back, Hannah! by Marisabina Russo. Greenwillow Books, 2001. Hannah is a toddler who loves to crawl all over the house, sometimes momentarily out of Mama's sight. Her mother jokingly tells Hannah that she's faster than a "crab on the beach," "mouse in the field," "lizard on a tree," and a "bunny in the garden." Encourage audience members to chime the title phrase every time Hannah crawls away from her Mama.

Diary of a Worm by Doreen Cronin, illustrated by Harry Bliss. Scholastic, 2003. This is a hilarious look at the world from a young worm's point of view. Worms may not be fast, but they love to say "Good morning" to ants (all 600 of them), eat garbage, scare human kids, and play with their spider friends (even if that spider friend claims you need legs to go fast). The highlight of the book is when several worms play "The Hokey Pokey." "You put your head in. You put your head out. You do the hokey pokey and you turn yourself about. That's all we could do." Cronin succeeds in making kids relate to this particular worm.

Fire! Fire! Hurry! Hurry! by Andrea Zimmerman and David Clemesha, illustrated by Karen Barbour. Greenwillow Books, 2003. This picture book shows how firefighters' lives can be slow one minute and hurried the next. A crew of firefighters settles down for a spaghetti dinner when the alarm goes off. They hurry to put out the fire and then drive back to the station. The alarm goes off again before they can enjoy their meal. This occurs over and over. There are several sound effects from the alarm's "Ding! Ding! Ding! Ding!" to the "Woooooo" of the fire truck.

Just Think by Bette Killion, illustrated by Linda Bronson. HarperCollins, 2001. This poetic text shows a girl thinking of fast things like hummingbird wings, lazy things like a "plump pig rolling," and still things like "snow drifting high." Ask the audience members for other items that fall under the headings of fast, lazy, and quiet things.

Score One for the Sloths by Helen Lester, illustrated by Lynn Munsinger. Houghton Mifflin, 2001. The sloth gang is hanging around Sleepy Valley Sloth School. They do their yawning, snoring, and rolling over lessons every once in awhile. Encourage your audience to join the sloth students in these activities. Sparky, a new sloth who is a "mover and a shaker," arrives. She cleverly saves the day when a representative of The Society for Organizing Sameness (SOS) threatens to close the school.

Turtle's Race with Beaver by Joseph and James Bruchac, illustrated by Jose Aruego and Ariane Dewey. Dial, 2003. Turtle races Beaver for the rights of the pond. Clever Turtle clamps down on Beaver's tail and goes for a ride. As they approach the finish line, Turtle bites down hard to cause Beaver to flip him ahead to win. The audience can participate by rooting along with the forest animals: "Turtle! Beaver! Turtle! Beaver!"

Zoom! by Robert Munsch, illustrated by Michael Martchenko. Scholastic, 2003. Lauretta doesn't want the slower model wheelchairs. She wants the "nice, new 92-speed, black, silver, and red, dirt-bike wheelchair." She gives it a test drive and when she puts it into twentieth gear, it goes "Zooooooooooom!" She even gets a speeding ticket. When Lauretta's brother has an accident (which is quite hilarious when you focus on the illustration and not the text), she drives him to the hospital on her powerful wheelchair. In the end, she complains that even this wheelchair is too slow. The audience members get a gander at the next huge wheelchair in the last illustration.

Old (And Not So Old) Favorites

The Gingerbread Boy by Paul Galdone. Clarion Books, 1975.

Go Dog Go by P. D. Eastman. Beginner Books, 1961.

The Great Turtle Drive by Steve Sanfield, illustrated by Dirk Zimmer. Knopf, 1996.

Hooray for Snail by John Stadler. Crowell, 1984.

Inch by Inch by Leo Lionni. Obolensky, 1960.

Molasses Flood by Blair Lent. Houghton Mifflin, 1992.

Quick, Quack, Quick by Marsha Arnold, illustrated by Lisa McCue. Random House, 1996.

The Tortoise and the Hare by Janet Stevens. Holiday House, 1984.

The Tortoise and the Jackrabbit by Susan Lowell, illustrated by Jim Harris. Northland, 1994.

Tortoise Brings the Mail by Dee Lillegard, illustrated by Jillian Lund. Dutton Children's Books, 1997.

Sweet Tooth

There are a great number of picture books about food on the market. This theme focuses on a popular food choice: sweets. You may want to take into consideration that some children cannot have sweets and add stories and activities about other food groups into this program, especially if you distribute treats afterwards.

Picture Book

Little Pea by Amy Krouse Rosenthal, illustrated by Jen Corace. Chronicle Books, 2005. Ironically, the first story in this program on sweets features the "much reviled pea." (It's surprising how many picture books show kids disliking peas. Bill Grossman's picture book *My Little Sister Ate One Hare* is just one example.) The twist to this story is that Little Pea hates to eat his candy. Papa Pea encourages Little Pea to eat the candy so that Little Pea will "grow up to be a big strong pea." To reward Little Pea, his parents give him his favorite dessert: spinach.

Poem

"Send My Spinach" by Douglas Florian from *Hot Potato: Mealtime Rhymes*, edited by Neil Philip and illustrated by Claire Henley. Clarion Books, 2004. This poem about spinach is a nice tie-in to the picture book *Little Pea*. In the poem, a child wants to send his

spinach to Spain on a train, on a boat, or by mail. This collection compiled by Philip is one of the best food-related poetry books ever. It contains several of my all-time favorite food poems, including "Yellow Butter" by Mary Ann Hoberman, "My Mouth" by Arnold Adoff, and "Baby's Drinking Song" by James Kirkup (which I recite at all of my

storytelling performances). Other poems from this collection that fit the "Sweet Tooth" theme include: "The Friendly Cinnamon Bun" by Russell Hoban; "Me, Myself, and I" (anonymous); "Oh, My Goodness, Oh, My Dear" by Clyde Watson; "Rice Pudding" by A. A. Milne; "The Spoon" by Elizabeth Fleming; and "Cake Mistake" by Douglas Florian, which appears later in this program.

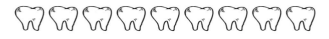

Picture Book

More Pies! by Robert Munsch, illustrated by Michael Martchenko. Scholastic, 2002. Samuel is hungry and the bowls of cereal, milk shakes, pancakes, and fried chicken that he eats for breakfast fail to satisfy him. He heads to the fair and enters a pie-eating contest. He bests a fireman, a lumberjack, and a construction worker before heading home with first prize: a gigantic pie. Beforehand, teach the audience to chant the much-repeated sound of Samuel and the others eating: "Chuka-chuka-chuka—Chuka-chuka-chuka—CHOMP!"

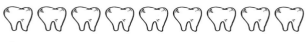

Fingerplay

"The Chocolate Chant"
Anonymous

Several early child-care providers taught me this fun fingerplay.

> Chocolate, chocolate,
> Tastes so sweet, *(Rub tummy.)*
> How much chocolate can I eat?
>
> Chocolate pudding, *(Hold up one finger.)*
> Chocolate chips, *(Two fingers.)*
> Chocolate ice cream double-dip. *(Three fingers.)*

> Chocolate candy, *(Four fingers.)*
> Chocolate bars, *(Five fingers.)*
> Chocolate cookies in a cookie jar. *(Six fingers.)*
>
> Chocolate syrup, *(Seven fingers.)*
> Chocolate drops, *(Eight fingers.)*
> Chocolate in my lollipops. *(Nine fingers.)*
>
> Chocolate cream pie, *(Ten fingers.)*
> Chocolate shake.
> *(Wiggle all ten fingers and shake body.)*
> Too much chocolate,
> Gives me a tummy ache!

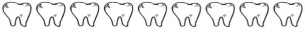

Picture Book

Otto Has a Birthday Party by Todd Parr. Little, Brown, and Company, 2004. Parr's picture books are deceptively hilarious for all ages. Otto the dog is making his own birthday cake. He adds "a cup of flour, two shoes, three bones, some pepperoni, a cootie bug, and a hot dog" and then spreads mud on top of the cake for frosting. The cake explodes in the oven. Luckily, an ice cream truck comes along. In the end, both Otto and author Parr warn the reader not to add "a cootie bug or a shoe in your cake."

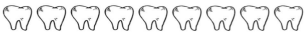

Felt Story

"The Sixteen-Scoop Ice Cream Cone"
by Rob Reid

Place a cone-shaped felt piece at the bottom of the felt board. Add different colored felt "scoops" above the cone each time a different flavor is mentioned in the story until there is a towering "Sixteen-Scoop Ice Cream Cone."

> I love ice cream. One day I went to an ice cream store that advertised sixteen different flavors. I couldn't make up my mind. So I ordered one of each.

On a sugar cone …

I had a scoop of Raspberry Road and
A scoop of Rocky Ripple and
A scoop of Blueberry Bliss and
A scoop of Magical Mint and
A scoop of Strawberry Surprise and
A scoop of Grape Jubilee and
A scoop of Rainbow Ice and
A scoop of Chocolate Chunky Chip and
A scoop of Cardinal Cherry Royale and
A scoop of Luscious Lime Sherbet and
A scoop of Black Licorice Delight and
A scoop of Okey-Dokey Mocha and
A scoop of Choco-Cherry Caramel Twist and
A scoop of Marshmallow Banana Butterscotch Blonde Blitz and
A scoop of Peanut Butter Bubblegum
    Crème Supreme.

The person behind the counter handed me my ice cream cone.

It had one, two, three, four, five, six, seven, eight, nine, ten, eleven, twelve, thirteen, fourteen, fifteen scoops.

"Fifteen scoops?" I said. "I thought you advertised sixteen flavors!"

"We do," said the person behind the counter. "But the sixteenth flavor is vanilla. We keep it in the back because nobody ever orders vanilla."

"Vanilla!" I screamed. "You have vanilla?" It's my favorite! Take back all of these other flavors and give me vanilla!"

So the person behind the counter took back the scoop of …

Peanut Butter Bubblegum Crème Supreme
    and
The scoop of Marshmallow Banana
    Butterscotch Blonde Blitz and
The scoop of Choco-Cherry Caramel Twist
    and
The scoop of Okey-Dokey Mocha and
The scoop of Black Licorice Delight and
The scoop of Luscious Lime Sherbet and
The scoop of Cardinal Cherry Royale and
The scoop of Chocolate Chunky Chip and
The scoop of Rainbow Ice and
The scoop of Grape Jubilee and
The scoop of Strawberry Surprise and
The scoop of Magical Mint and
The scoop of Blueberry Bliss and
The scoop of Rocky Ripple and
The scoop of Raspberry Road.

And then the person behind the counter gave me a vanilla ice cream cone.

A sixteen-scoop vanilla ice cream cone!

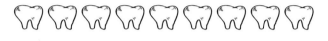

Picture Book

Ruby Bakes a Cake by Susan Hill, illustrated by Margie Moore. HarperCollins, 2004. Ruby Raccoon wants to bake a cake, but doesn't know how. Various animal friends tell her what to put into her cake. Squirrel tells her to add nuts. Bunny Rabbit suggests carrot tops. Dan Ducks tells her slugs. Jenny Wren suggests wiggly worms. Frankie Frog advises to add flies. Ruby returns to her kitchen and adds these ingredients to her cake. Even though she invites her friends over to eat it, she's worried that it doesn't look good. Her friends do a nice job of making her feel good about her cake. The audience members will be sure to add appropriate sound effects when they hear which ingredients are going into the cake.

Poem

"Cake Mistake" by Douglas Florian from *Hot Potato: Mealtime Rhymes.* This short poem describes a mother who mistakenly adds glue to her cake batter. The kids "chewandchewandchew."

Picture Book

Fortune Cookie Fortunes by Grace Lin. Knopf, 2004. A Chinese American girl and her family crack open their fortune cookies after a delicious meal. The next day, the girl notices that all of the fortunes that they read are coming true. The girl's own fortune reads "You will see the world in a different way." There are many fortunes scattered throughout the text. Don't worry about reading them all to your audience (although some audience members may insist). The girl reads another fortune that tells her "Look forward to a life of great fortune." The back endpaper has the following fortune: "You have just read a good book." Indeed.

As the children exit the program area, give each one a wrapped fortune cookie (available for purchase from many Asian food stores). Encourage them to open their fortune cookies at home with their families. Otherwise, you may have several broken pieces of cookies and slips of paper to clean up (I speak from experience).

Backup Picture Books

Arnie the Doughnut by Laurie Keller. Henry Holt & Company, 2003. Don't let the text-heavy book, with the many sidebars, stop you from sharing this picture book with the kids. Stick to the main narrative of Arnie, a doughnut who is shocked to learn that he is to be eaten. The dialogue between Arnie and Mr. Bing, the man who bought him from the bakery (where the other doughnuts are delighted by the thought of being eaten), is hilarious. In the end,

Arnie becomes Mr. Bing's pet doughnut-dog. Arnie is especially good at rolling over. Don't miss the final illustration that shows a "Beware of DOuGhnut" sign.

Beverly Billingsly Takes the Cake by Alexander Stadler. Harcourt, 2005. Beverly decides to bake a birthday cake for Oliver. Unfortunately, she forgets to grease the pan and the cake is ruined. Fortunately, Beverly's mother comes up with a clever way to salvage the mess, by turning the broken pieces into butterfly wings. After Beverly finishes decorating the butterfly cake, she receives requests from friends to make cakes for their birthday parties.

Cookie Count: A Tasty Pop-Up by Robert Sabuda. Simon & Schuster, 1997. Sabuda is a master at creating elaborate paper-engineered books. These pop-ups begin with "1 Chocolate Chip Cookie" and end with "10 Gingerbread Windows." There are several types of pop-up cookie pictures in-between that look good enough to eat.

Gingerbread Baby by Jan Brett. Putnam, 1999. Matti opens the oven door too soon. Instead of a completed gingerbread boy, out pops a gingerbread baby who proceeds to lead a host of animals and humans on a long chase. While everyone is trying to catch the tasty treat, Matti creates a gingerbread house and provides a safe haven for the gingerbread baby. The final illustration contains a lift-the-flap, which reveals the happy occupant of the gingerbread house.

Mmm, Cookies! by Robert Munsch, illustrated by Michael Martchenko. Scholastic, 2000. Mean-spirited Christopher molds play clay into a cookie shape. He offers it to his mother. She takes a bite and yells "Yuck!

Pwah! Splicht! Play Clay! Gla-Gla-Gla-Gla!" Christopher does the same thing to his father. Eventually, Christopher learns his lesson and bakes a real cookie for his parents (even though it's the size of a boulder). This story features Munsch's trademark irreverent humor, yet the various sound effects make this a delight to read aloud.

Scaredy Mouse by Alan MacDonald, illustrated by Tim Warnes. Tiger Tales, 2002. Nibbles and her younger mouse brother, Squeak, sneak through the house in search of "a chocolate cake as big as a wheel." Squeak is terrified of running into the cat. He runs away from various objects he believes are the cat. When the two mice finally find the cake, the cat attacks. Fortunately for the mice, the cat becomes tangled in string and Squeak overcomes his fear (and enjoys his chocolate cake, too).

The Trial of Cardigan Jones by Tim Egan. Houghton Mifflin, 2004. Cardigan the moose stops to inspect Mrs. Brown's homemade apple pie. When the pie is missing, everyone suspects Cardigan. During the trial, Cardigan repeatedly knocks things over with his unwieldy antlers, including the judge. The wise judge has a hunch and leads everyone to the scene of the crime. They find the missing pie in the bushes below Mrs. Brown's window, where Cardigan had inadvertently knocked it over. The jury finds Cardigan not guilty and joins him for a piece of Mrs. Brown's pie (even though he breaks her vase in the end).

Turnover Tuesday by Phyllis Root, illustrated by Helen Craig. Candlewick Press, 1998. Bonnie Bumble eats five plum turnovers and turns upside down. She does her chores, such as milking the cow and gathering the eggs, upside down. This leads to disastrous results. She returns home, eats the sixth turnover, and turns right side up. Unfortunately, her dog laps up the crumbs and flips over himself.

Old (And Not So Old) Favorites

The Baker's Dozen: A Colonial American Tale by Heather Forest, illustrated by Susan Gaber. Harcourt, 1988.

Bread and Jam for Frances by Russell Hoban, illustrated by Lillian Hoban. HarperCollins, 1964.

The Doorbell Rang by Pat Hutchins. Greenwillow Books, 1986.

Garth Pig and the Ice Cream Lady by Mary Rayner. Atheneum, 1977.

Giant Jam Sandwich by John Vernon Lord. Houghton Mifflin, 1972.

How to Make an Apple Pie and See the World by Marjorie Priceman. Knopf, 1994.

Ice Cream Soup by Frank Modell. Greenwillow Books, 1988.

Jam Day by Barbara Joosse, illustrated by Emily Arnold McCully. Harper, 1987.

Max's Chocolate Chicken by Rosemary Wells. Dial, 1989.

Mr. Putter and Tabby Pick the Pears by Cynthia Rylant, illustrated by Arthur Howard. Harcourt, 1995.

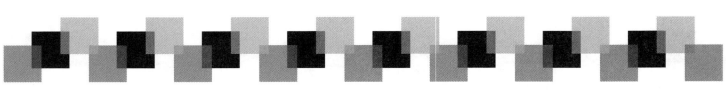

Toyland

Decorate the program area with toys, such as teddy bears, dolls, cars, and action figures. Place the toys where they can be seen, but not within reach of the children. These toys will not only set the atmosphere for the theme, but will also be featured in one of the activities. Storyteller's tip: You can choose virtually any fingerplay or song to include in a toy-related theme program. Simply have dolls represent any fingerplay or song that features people; stuffed animals for those activities featuring the animal kingdom; toy trucks/trains/cars for fingerplays and songs featuring transportation; and so on.

Picture Book

I Lost My Bear by Jules Feiffer. William Morrow & Co., 1998. A girl loses her bear and begs her family to help locate it. They give her clues on how to go about finding it. She discovers several other items she had previously lost, but fails to find her bear. She loses her composure at bedtime. The line, "I c-c-c-c-could-couldn't finnnnnd her becauuuuse yooooouuuuuuuuu would-would-wouldn't hellllllllp meeeeeeeeee" is particularly fun to read aloud. It turns out that the bear was in the girl's bed the whole time.

Musical Activity

"Down by the Bay"
Traditional

Sing or recite this popular traditional nonsense song and adapt it to feature the toys decorating the program area. The traditional words go like this:

> Down by the bay,
> Where the watermelons grow,
> Back to my home, I dare not go,
> For if I do, my mother will say,
> **"Did you ever see a bear combing his hair,**
> Down by the bay?"

> Down by the bay,
> Where the watermelons grow,
> Back to my home, I dare not go,
> For if I do, my mother will say,
> **"Did you ever see a moose kissing a goose,**
> Down by the bay?"

Add new verses, replacing the bold phrases with new silly rhymes featuring the toys in the program area. For example:

"Did you ever see a bunny eating honey?"

"Did you ever see a dog hopping like a frog?"

"Did you ever see a toy car driving into a star?"

"Did you ever see a dolly sounding jolly?"

"Did you ever see a rubber duckie driving a truckie?"

(Make up your own verses or ask the audience members to create new lines.)

"Down by the Bay" can be found on the following children's musical recordings:

- *Country Goes Raffi.* Rounder, 2001.

- *Nancy Cassidy's Kids Songs: The Sing-Along Songbook* (with CD) by Nancy Cassidy. Klutz, 2004.

- *101 Toddler Favorites.* Music for Little People, 2003.

- *Playing Favorites* by Greg and Steve. Youngheart, 1991.

- *Raffi on Broadway* by Raffi. MCA, 1993.

- *Singable Songs for the Very Young* by Raffi. Rounder, 1976.

This fun song has also been turned into a picture book based on Raffi's version—*Down by the Bay* by Raffi, illustrated by Nadine Bernard Westcott (Crown Publishers, 1987).

Picture Book

Knuffle Bunny by Mo Willems. Hyperion, 2004. Tiny tot Trixie and her father take the family laundry and Trixie's stuffed rabbit Knuffle Bunny to the neighborhood Laundromat. When Knuffle Bunny goes missing, Trixie tries to tell her father, but all that comes out is gibberish. It's Mom who finally realizes that Trixie is trying to tell her parents that Knuffle Bunny is missing. Once they locate the bunny, Trixie proudly says her first words: "Knuffle Bunny." I had the pleasure of meeting Mo Willems who told me that the title character's name is pronounced "Kuh-nuffle."

Movement Activity

"Zoom Zoom Zoom"
Traditional

Have the children stand up and act out the lyrics.

Zoom Zoom Zoom,
Hear the airplane engines sing.
Zoom Zoom Zoom,
See it fly with outspread wings.

Zoom Zoom Zoom,
Watch it turn and then swoop down.
Zoom Zoom Zoom,
Soon it lands down on the ground.

Picture Book

Olivia ... and the Missing Toy by Ian Falconer. Atheneum, 2003. Olivia's toy goes missing. After searching the entire house and questioning her siblings (to which baby brother

William replies "Wooshee gaga"), Olivia discovers that Perry the dog "chewed it to bits." Falconer's humor works especially well for intergenerational audiences with the older audience members appreciating the photo of dancer Martha Graham gracing one wall, and the inclusion of Edward George Bulwer-Lytton's infamous line "It was a dark and stormy night."

Movement Activity

"I Like to Be a Jumping Jack"
Traditional; have the children stand up and act out the lyrics.

> I like to be a jumping jack,
> And jump out from a box.
> I like to be a rocking horse,
> And rock and rock and rock.
> I like to be a spinning top,
> And spin and spin and spin.
> I like to be a rubber ball,
> And bounce way up and down.

Picture Book

Matthew's Truck by Katherine Ayres, illustrated by Hideko Takahashi. Candlewick Press, 2005. Matthew imagines himself behind the wheels of his yellow and red toy truck driving up hills (stairs), enormous mountains (the sofa), into deep lakes (a fish tank), under bridges (a chair), and finally "into its own private parking place" (Matthew's bed).

Movement Activity

"Playground Time"
by Rob Reid

This activity works best in an area with a big open space. Have the children stand up in a large circle or a few smaller circles and follow the directions. There is a lot of up and down movement, so feel free to read the rhymes slowly with plenty of pauses.

> All join hands, *(Join hands.)*
> Circle around,
> Now you have,
> A merry-go-round. *(Move in a circle.)*
>
> Next sit down,
> *(Allow the children to find a seat.)*
> Shout and sing,
> *("Yippee" or "La-la-la" usually works.)*
> Legs out front, *(Sit with legs out front.)*
> Arms up—swing!
> *(Arms overhead—mime swinging back and forth.)*
>
> Hula hoop, *(Stand and swing hips.)*
> Bumper cars, *(Bump hips with neighbor.)*
> Teeter totter, *(Face neighbor and hold hands. Take turns going up and down.)*
> Monkey bars.
> *(Hands overhead and mime moving along bars.)*
>
> Balance beam,
> *(Mime walking on a narrow beam.)*
> Slippery slide,
> *(Sit and hold hands up slightly behind head.)*
> Crawl through tunnels, *(Crawl a few steps.)*
> Rocking-horse ride.
> *(Sit and rock back and forth.)*
>
> Catch the ball, *(Mime catching a ball.)*
> Dance and rhyme, *(Stand and dance in place.)*
> Imagination,
> Playground time! *(Arms outstretched.)*

Toy Book

Tails by Matthew Van Fleet. Harcourt, 2003. End the program by showing the audience how some books are actually toys themselves. Van Fleet's creation is one of the most playful toy books on the market. Let the children feel the furry tiger tail and the bumpy alligator tail. Let them take turns lifting flaps that reveal peacock's shiny tail and pull the lever to see monkeys pulling other monkeys by their tails. Be careful with the scratch-and-sniff skunk's tail! The last feature is a huge whale's tail spread over four pages. The text is short, but you'll spend a lot of time with this book.

Backup Picture Books

Albert the Bear by Nick Butterworth. HarperCollins, 2002. The toys in Mr. Jolly's toy shop are worried about the new teddy bear. He appears sad. They come up with several ideas to cheer him up. Many of these attempts end in disaster. Butterworth slips in several toy and cartoon characters that your sharpest eyes in the audience will note, including Bob the Builder, Waldo from Where's Waldo, Paddington the Bear, Kipper, Raymond Briggs's Snowman, and more.

Bath Time by Eileen Spinelli, illustrated by Janet Pedersen. Cavendish, 2003. This predictable book is fun to read aloud. The penguin child loves to take baths, as long as he can add his favorite toys. A boat, a porpoise, a shark, a snake, a whale, a beach ball, a water pistol, and other items (including mother's jewelry) go in the tub. Of course, at the end, there's no room for the penguin child in the bathtub.

Bunny Party by Rosemary Wells. Viking, 2001. Max and Ruby set up for Grandma's party. They argue about which "guests" (toys) to invite. Ruby wants Rapunzel, Curly Shirley, Tooth Fairy, Mr. and Mrs. Quack, Pinocchio, and Walky-Talky Bear. Max prefers Jellybelly Shooter Spider, Ear-Splitter Space Cadet, and Can't-Sit-Up Slug. The audience will have fun watching Max carry out his scheme.

Elizabeti's Doll by Stephanie Stuve-Bodeen, illustrated by Christy Hale. Lee & Low Books, 1998. Set in an African village, Elizabeti watches her mother take care of the new baby. Not having a doll and wanting to care for a baby herself, Elizabeti picks up a large rock and names it Eva. Elizabeti "bathes" Eva, "feeds" Eva, and carries Eva around in "a bright cloth called a kanga." Elizabeti worries when Eva goes missing.

Farmer Will by Jane Cowen-Fletcher. Candlewick Press, 2001. Will takes his toy farm animals—"his horse Orsey, his cow Dow, his sheep Bah, and his pig Wink-Wink"—outside to play. Once out of the house, they stretch into life-size animals (at least in Will's imagination). They all play Hide-and-Seek, Catch-Me-If-You-Can, Stomp-in-the-Mud, Run-through-the-Sprinkler, and Ring-Around-the-Rosy before shrinking back into Will's hat to take a rest.

Good Night, Hattie, My Dearie, My Dove by Alice Schertle, illustrated by Ted Rand. HarperCollins, 2002. Hattie counts ten of her toys and dolls, many now tattered and dirty from heavy use. After leading them in a parade, Hattie asks her parents to bring them to her in bed one by one. Teach the audience to recite the title phrase, something that Hattie's Mama and Daddy say over and over.

Plaidypus Lost by Janet Stevens and Susan Stevens Crummel. Holiday House, 2004. A girl consistently loses her stuffed toy "Plaidypus" at the park, the grocery store, the beach, and on a car ride. After the last misadventure, the girl's grandmother repairs the torn Plaidypus into a "new one-eyed, one-armed Plaida-Polka-Stripus." The audience will chant along with the book's refrain: "Plaidypus lost / Plaidypus found / This story goes around and around."

Platypus and the Lucky Day by Chris Riddell. Harcourt, 2002. Platypus is having lots of bad luck beginning when his kite gets stuck in a tree. He decides to paint, but the weather turns bad and ruins his picture. After taking a break, he finds other toys to brighten up his day. It appears as if more bad luck is on the way when Platypus crashes his go-cart into a tree and the kite lands in his lap.

Please DO Feed the Bears by Phyllis Reynolds Naylor, illustrated by Ana López Escrivá. Atheneum, 2002. Percy accidentally sabotages his family's beach picnic by replacing the food with his different teddy bears. By the end, he comes up with a scheme to feed his family and prolong their trip.

Sammy and the Dinosaurs by Ian Whybrow, illustrated by Adrian Reynolds. Orchard Books, 1999. Sammy loves his toy dinosaurs because he can fix them, bathe them, and take them to bed. He panics when he loses them on a train, but convinces the man at the lost and found that they are indeed his as he recites their names: "Scelidosaurus, Stegosaurus, Triceratops…" The book ends with the inscription "Endosaurus."

Old (And Not So Old) Favorites

Are You There, Bear? by Ron Maris. Greenwillow Books, 1984.

Corduroy by Don Freeman. Viking, 1968.

Dogger by Shirley Hughes. Lothrop, Lee & Shepard Books, 1988.

The Marvelous Toy by Tom Paxton, illustrated by Elizabeth Sayles. Morrow, 1996.

Poppy, the Panda by Dick Gackenbach. Clarion Books, 1984.

Tom and Pippo Go for a Walk by Helen Oxenbury. McMillan, 1988.

William, the Vehicle King by Laura Newton, illustrated by Jacqueline Rogers. Bradbury, 1987.

Great Toy Books

Since toy books are toys themselves (or toy-like in nature), they are natural additions to the toy theme. Many children's book creators specialize in designing toy books. These include Rod Campbell, Eric Carle, David Carter, Lois Ehlert, Eric Hill, Chuck Murphy, Jan Pienkowski, and Robert Sabuda. Check out their individual titles, as well as the following favorites:

Baby Danced the Polka by Karen Beaumont, illustrated by Jennifer Plecas. Dial, 2004.

Bluebird's Nest by Dorothea DePrisco, illustrated by Jo Parry and designed by Melanie Random. Piggy Toes Press, 2005.

Bunny Mail: A Max and Ruby Lift-the-Flap Book by Rosemary Wells. Viking, 2004.

Doors by Roxie Munro. SeaStar, 2004.

Inside Freight Train by Donald Crews. HarperFestival, 2001.

Jazzy in the Jungle by Lucy Cousins. Candlewick Press, 2002.

Knick-Knack Paddywhack! by Paul O. Zelinsky. Dutton Children's Books, 2002.

The Monster Who Loved Books by Keith Faulkner, illustrated by Jonathan Lambert. Orchard Books, 2002.

Peek-a-Zoo! by Marie Torres Cimarusti, illustrated by Stephanie Peterson. Dutton, 2003.

Toes, Ears and Nose by Marion Dane Bauer, illustrated by Karen Katz. Little Simon, 2003.

Uh-Oh! A Lift-the-Flap Story by Marion Dane Bauer, illustrated by Valeria Petrone. Little Simon, 2002.

The Wheels on the Bus by Paul O. Zelinsky. Dutton Children's Books, 1990.

The Wide-Mouthed Frog by Keith Faulkner, illustrated by Jonathan Lambert. Dial, 1996.

Way Out West

Dress up in your blue jeans, bandanna, and cowboy hat as you share stories and activities about cowboys and cowgirls. Play recordings by Gene Autrey, Roy Rogers and Dale Evans, Riders in the Sky, or Michael Martin Murphy—all of whom sing traditional cowboy songs. Ask the children to sit "around the campfire" to hear some tales from the Wild West.

Picture Books

Lasso Lou and Cowboy McCoy by Barbara Larmon Failing, illustrated by Tedd Arnold. Dial, 2003. This extremely silly story is a good one with which to start off the program as the audience members learn about becoming a cowboy along with the main character. Cowboy McCoy mistakenly ropes the Bo-Dee-Oh Ranch foreman, Smelly Mel (along with a chicken and a pig). McCoy also tries to name his horse "SundayMondayTuesdayWednesdayThursdayFridaySaturday" until Lasso Lou tells him to pick a shorter name. Cowboy McCoy picks his favorite day—"Payday."

Sixteen Cows by Lisa Wheeler, illustrated by Kurt Cyrus. Harcourt, 2002. Cowboy Gene owns eight cows with names such as Mudskipper and Twinkle Toes. Cowgirl Sue owns eight cows, too. Their names include Jelly Roll and Peekaboo. Gene and Sue have side-by-side ranches. When the herds get mixed together after a twister, the two try to separate the cows with "come-home" songs. Eventually, Cowboy Gene and Cowgirl Sue get married and the 16 cows serve as bridesmaids. For added fun, sing the "come-home" songs (which consist of the 16 cow names) with a little off-key twang.

Rhyme

"I Know a Cowboy, I Know a Cowgirl"
by Rob Reid

This silly little rhyme works as a nice accompanying activity between the Wheeler picture book and the following Charlip book. Recite it to the kids and pause before the last word of each verse, so that the kids can make the appropriate animal noise.

> I know a Cowboy named Gene,
> I know a Cowgirl named Sue,
> They're in charge of a herd of cows,
> The cows go "Moo!"
>
> I know a Horseboy named Hank,
> I know a Horsegirl named Renee,
> They're in charge of a herd of horses,
> The horses go "Neigh!"
>
> I know a Snakeboy named Sam,
> I know a Snakegirl named Miss,
> They're in charge of a herd of snakes,
> The snakes go "Hiss!"
>
> I know a Coyoteboy named Gene,
> I know a Coyotegirl named Lou,
> They're in charge of a herd of coyotes,
> The coyotes go, "Arrrrrooooo!"

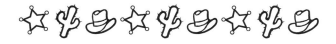

Picture Book

Little Old Big Beard and Big Young Little Beard by Remy Charlip, illustrated by Charlip and Tamara Rettenmund. Marshall Cavendish, 2003. This hilarious book features a short older cowboy with a long beard and a tall young cowboy with a short beard. The tall page format emphasizes the size difference between the two along with the mountainous ride they have as they search for their one cow Grace. At the end, after Grace finds the two cowboys, they sing "A-Grazing Grace / How sweet you found / Such wretched souls as we…" Belt it out!

Picture Book/Song

Home on the Range by Brian Ajhar. Dial, 2004. This picture book features several verses of the traditional cowboy song. Sing the text of the well-known first verse.

> Oh, give me a home,
> Where the buffalo roam,
> Where the deer and the antelope play.
>
> Where seldom is heard,
> A discouraging word,
> And the skies are not cloudy all day.
>
> Home, home on the range.
> Where the deer and the antelope play.
> Where seldom is heard,
> A discouraging word,
> And the skies are not cloudy all day.

While singing, show all of the pictures in Ajhar's book, which feature a city child in a western-themed bedroom. The small boy sees the antelope in the clouds above the city, and the Wild West in his dreams. Teach this simple song to your young audience. They will learn it quickly. For all of the silliness I employ in my story programs, one of my favorite memories as a storyteller is when a group of preschoolers sang this song with me in hushed tones.

Picture Book

Sing, Sophie! by Dayle Ann Dodds, illustrated by Rosanne Litzinger. Candlewick

Press, 1997. Here's another chance to sing for those storytellers who don't mind being loud and boisterous (and silly). Sophie, who dresses like a cowgirl, loves to sing at the top of her voice. The rest of her family tells her to sing somewhere else. Finally, they all realize that Sophie's singing is the only thing that'll stop Baby Jacob from crying. So go ahead, belt out Sophie's lines; the more off-key, the better. "My legs are skinny / my toes are fat / I've got the temper of a tiger cat / But I'm a cowgirl, don't you know / Yippee-ky-yee! Yippee-ky-yo!"

Movement Activity

"I'm a Little Cowboy"
Anonymous

This variation of "I'm a Little Teapot" was found on several early childhood Web sites and can be done again as "I'm a Little Cowgirl."

> I'm a little cowboy, *(Point to self.)*
> Here is my hat, *(Point to head.)*
> Here are my spurs, *(Point to heels.)*
> And here are my chaps. *(Point to legs.)*
>
> As soon as I wake up, *(Stretch and yawn.)*
> I work all day long.
> *(Mime twirling a lasso overhead.)*
> I get on my horse,
> *(Mime throwing a leg over a horse.)*
> And ride along. *(Gallop around the room.)*

Picture Book

Armdadilly Chili by Helen Ketteman, illustrated by Will Terry. Albert Whitman, 2004.

This retelling of "The Little Red Hen" is set in the Southwest. Miss Billie Armadilly goes through the steps to make a pot of her special "armadilly chili." She asks for help from a tarantula named Tex, Mackie the Bluebird, and a horned toad known as Taffy. After refusing to help, they see the error of their ways and bring along a thermos of hot apple cider, hot jalapeno biscuits, and a box of chocolate fudge to go along with Miss Billie's ingredients (beetles, jalapeno and chipotle chilies, and prickly pear cactus). This book lends itself to the use of homemade felt characters of the different food items listed in the book, along with a gathering basket and a pot.

Picture Book

Cowboy Dreams by Kathi Appelt, illustrated by Barry Root. HarperCollins, 1999. As a young boy falls asleep, he dreams of heading for camp with the other cowboys. They all listen to Camp Cookie sing an evening lullaby around the campfire. As the cowboys head for their bedrolls, coyotes add a "Yip yip yaroo" to the young cowboy's dreams. End the program by having the audience make a hushed coyote howl as they exit the story program area to a recording of "Happy Trails," which can be found on the following musical recordings:

- *The Cowboy Album.* Kid Rhino, 1992.

- *Jeremiah was a Bullfrog* by Hoyt Axton. Youngheart Music, 1995.

- *When the Rain Comes Down* by Cathy Fink. Rounder, 1988.

A good alternative recording is "Cowgirl's Lullaby" which can be found on *Blanket Full of Dreams* by Cathy Fink and Marcy Marxer (Rounder, 1996).

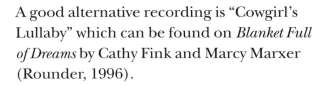

Backup Picture Books

Armadillo Tattletale by Helen Ketteman, illustrated by Keith Graves. Scholastic, 2000. In the old days, Armadillos had ears as "tall as jack rabbits." Armadillo uses his large ears to eavesdrop on private conversations. He repeats these conversations, but doesn't convey them correctly, causing many hard feelings. Alligator angrily chomps Armadillo's ears. That's why, to this day, armadillos have "tiny, teeny, itsy, weenie, little ears."

Covered Wagon, Bumpy Trails by Verla Kay, illustrated by S. D. Schindler. Putnam, 2000. Panoramic, double-page spreads accompany a simple rhyme to show the hardships of crossing the West in covered wagons. The audience will get a good sense of the treacherous times pioneers faced as they traversed the Great Plains and the Rocky Mountains on their way to California. This is a deceptively popular book with the preschool crowd.

Cowgirl Rosie and Her Five Baby Bison by Stephen Gulbis. Little, Brown, and Company, 2001. Cowgirl Rosie lives on a ranch with her five miniature bison: Bigwig, Bonnie, Beefy, Butch, and Baby B. The bison babies are kidnapped while on a trip to town. Sheriff Joe helps Cowgirl Rosie rescue the bison from Snakey Jake.

Hannah Mae O'Hannigan's Wild West Show by Lisa Campbell Ernst. Simon & Schuster, 2003. Hannah Mae lives in a city and wants to be a cowgirl. She wears "cowpoke duds" and practices cow herding with her pet hamsters. She saves the day, while visiting her uncle's ranch, when a large herd of stampeding hamsters bewilder and scare the real, grown-up cowboys.

Joe Cinders by Marianne Mitchell, illustrated by Bryan Langdo. Henry Holt & Company, 2002. This retelling of the Cinderella story shows the main character to be a poor cowboy who works hard all day while his stepbrothers lay around the ranch. After the stepbrothers head off for a fiesta at Rancho Milagro, a strange man changes a horse into a pickup truck and gives Joe new clothes, including a pair of red boots. Rosalinda finds a boot that Joe leaves behind and sets off in search of the rightful owner.

Ordinary Audrey by Peter Harris, illustrated by David Runert. Tiger Tales, 2001. Deadwood Deb is the toughest person in Deadwood, the toughest town of all. This five-year-old "could out-lasso, out-snarl, and out-eat even the toughest cowboy in the land." When Deadwood Deb goes on vacation, it's up to her twin sister Ordinary Audrey to save the town from outlaws. However, Ordinary Audrey "liked playing with teddy bears … and swinging on swings—just as long as they didn't go too high." The kids will enjoy learning how Ordinary Audrey saved the day to become known as "Extraordinary Audrey."

Pedro the Brave by Leo Broadley, illustrated by Holly Swain. Tiger Tales, 2002. A hungry wolf happens upon young Pedro, his dog, and his horse. The wolf threatens to eat them. Pedro tricks the wolf by suggesting that the wolf allow Pedro to make his own sauce before jumping in the pan. He mixes "Tabasco and whiskey and dynamite dust, gunpowder, garlic, and ham. Cactus, paprika, and vindaloo pastes, mustard, green chilies, and jam." Pedro offers the wolf a taste. Of course, the wolf shoots flames out of his mouth and decides to have ice cream instead.

A Wild Cowboy by Dana Kessimakis Smith, illustrated by Laura Freeman-Hines. Hyperion, 2004. An urban family pretends to experience the West on a trip to grandmother's place in this rhymed-verse picture book. The boy rides his horse whose "mane is silky black" (his mother). They round up the cattle (puppy dogs), and eat "some grub, some cowboy food" (popcorn, hot dogs, and juice boxes).

Old (And Not So Old) Favorites

The Cowboy and the Black-Eyed Pea by Tony Johnston, illustrated by Warren Ludwig. Putnam, 1992.

Cowboys by Glen Rounds. Holiday House, 1991.

Four Dollars and Fifty Cents by Eric Kimmel, illustrated by Glen Rounds. Holiday House, 1990.

The Golly Sisters Go West by Betsy Byars, illustrated by Sue Truesdell. Harper, 1985.

How I Spent My Summer Vacation by Mark Teague. Crown Publishers, 1995.

Iva Dunnit and the Big Wind by Carol Purdy, illustrated by Steven Kellogg. Dial, 1985.

Pecos Bill by Steven Kellogg. William Morrow & Co., 1986.

Welcome to Library Land

Who is the most important community member? Arguably, it's the librarian! What's the greatest invention in the world? Why, the library, of course. The following lesson plan features picture books and activities that celebrate the world of books and the folks who feature them in school media centers, bookstores, and public libraries. As the children enter the program area, play one of my favorite songs that features books: "Read a Book to Me" by Tom Pease on his recording *I'm Gonna Reach* (Tomorrow River Music, 1989). You can order this recording by visiting www.tompease.com.

Picture Books

Library Lil by Suzanne Williams, illustrated by Steven Kellogg. Dial, 1997. This picture book starts out with the line, "I bet you think all librarians are mousy little old ladies. Hair rolled up in bun." Library Lil breaks this stereotype in this tall tale about a librarian serving a community full of television lovers. Lil runs afoul of a motorcycle gang led by Bust-em-up Bill. After the big showdown, the gang becomes avid readers (getting into a fight over who gets to read *The Mouse and the Motorcycle*). The gang also reads several Steven Kellogg books.

Maisy Goes to the Library by Lucy Cousins. Candlewick Press, 2005. Maisy, the popu-

lar mouse, looks for a book about fish at her local public library. She notices that there are several things to do at the library, including using the computer, listening to music, and going to storytime. The characters get a big laugh out of the story about the old woman who swallowed a fly. "They were still laughing when they checked out their books and went outside to play."

Musical Activity

"Threw It Out the Window"
Traditional

This silly camp song favorite appears all over under several different titles. However, all versions feature popular nursery rhymes, which are found in every public and school library. You can add any nursery rhyme to the lyrics. Simply start off with a familiar nursery rhyme (sung slowly and quietly) and add the following words (while singing enthusiastically), "And he (she/they) threw it out the window, the window, the second story window …"

> Old King Cole,
> Was a merry old soul,
> And a merry old soul was he.
> He called for his pipe,
> And he called for his bowl and …
> He threw them out the window,
> The window, the window,
> The second story window.
> He called for his pipe,
> And he called for his bowl,
> And he threw them out the window!

> Mary had a little lamb,
> Its fleece was white as snow.
> And everywhere that Mary went …
> She threw it out the window,
> The window, the window,
> The second story window.
> And everywhere that Mary went,
> She threw it out the window!

> Jack and Jill went up a hill,
> To fetch a pail of water.
> Jack fell down and broke his crown …
> And threw it out the window,
> The window, the window,
> The second story window,
> Jack fell down and broke his crown
> And threw it out the window!

> The itsy-bitsy spider,
> Went up the waterspout.
> Down came the rain and …
> Threw him out the window,
> The window, the window,
> The second story window,
> Down came the rain
> And threw him out the window!

Solicit ideas from kids and add your own verses. You can find a musical version of "Out the Window" on the following recording:

* *Sing It! Say It! Stamp It! Sway It! Vol. 2* by Peter and Ellen Allard. Peter and Ellen Allard, 1999.

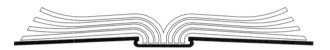

Picture Book

Beverly Billingsly Borrows a Book by Alexander Stadler. Harcourt, 2002. Beverly is excited to get her first library card at the Piedmont Public Library. She checks out a book titled *Dinosaurs of the Cretaceous Period*. She's so inspired by the book that "she couldn't put it down." She worries when she misses the due date. Her friends tell her that you have to pay a lot of money when it's late. "Oh, like a thousand dollars, I think." Her parents notice her worrying and help her return her overdue book to the library. Everything turns out well when the librarian introduces her to another kid who loves dinosaurs. Together, they form the Piedmont Dinosaur Club.

Poem

A Light in the Attic by Shel Silverstein. HarperCollins, 1981. Beverly Billingsly had a fear about overdue books. Share the poem "Overdue" from this popular poetry collection. The narrator is worried because "his library book is 42 / Years overdue." Afterwards, hold up any edition of *The Guinness Book of World Records* and inform your audience that the record for the longest overdue library book is 288 years!

Joke

"Bok! Bok!
Anonymous

Here's a short version of an old favorite joke shared over the years by librarians:

> "A chicken walks into the library and says, 'Bok!' *(Imitate the flapping of the chicken's wings as you say "Bok!" each time.)*
>
> The librarian shrugs her shoulder and tucks a book under one of the chicken's wings. The chicken leaves the library.
>
> A few moments later, the chicken returns, drops the book in front of the librarian, and says, 'Bok!'
>
> The librarian shrugs her shoulders and tucks another book under the chicken's wing. The chicken leaves the library.
>
> A few moments later, the chicken returns, drops the book in front of the librarian, and says, 'Bok!'
>
> The librarian tucks another book under the chicken's wing, but this time decides to follow the chicken.

The chicken leaves the front of the library, wanders down a path that goes to a nearby creek, and walks up to a frog.

The librarian sees the chicken prop the book in front of the frog. The frog looks at the cover of the book and, in a loud voice, croaks 'Read-It!'"

For those folks who are more comfortable reading a story than telling jokes, substitute the picture book version of the joke—*Book! Book! Book!* by Deborah Bruss, illustrated by Tiphanie Beeke (Scholastic, 2001). Several bored farm animals go in to the local library. The librarian fails to understand what the animals are saying. Finally, the chicken clucks, "Book!" The librarian gives the hen three books. The animals happily read the books back at the farm, except for the bullfrog who complains, "I already Read It! Read It, read, it, read it ..."

Poem

"A Book! Bok! Bok!"
by Rob Reid

The above joke inspired me to create this simple ditty.

> A book! Bok! Bok!
> A book! Bok! Bok!
> A chicken's got a book! Bok! Bok!
>
> *(Repeat each verse twice. Have the audience join you the second time. Eventually the kids will chime in the name of the animal based on the sound cue before you can say it.)*
>
> A book! Bow Wow!
> A book! Bow Wow!
> A dog has got a book! Bow Wow!

A book! Baa! Baa!
A book! Baa! Baa!
A sheep has got a book! Baa Baa!

A book! Buzz! Buzz!
A book! Buzz! Buzz!
A bee has got a book! Buzz! Buzz!

Add your own verses. The animal noise doesn't necessarily have to begin with a "B." I did this with a group of first graders and one kid volunteered the following:

A book! Burp! Burp!
A book! Burp! Burp!
A kid has got a book! Burp! Burp!

Picture Book

Wild About Books by Judy Sierra, illustrated by Marc Brown. Knopf, 2004. Librarian Molly McGrew mistakenly drives the bookmobile to the zoo. The books become a hit with the animals. They all become big readers. Some of the animals are inspired to write their own stories. The hippo even wins the Zoolitzer Prize! In the end, a Zoobrary is built.

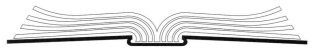

Musical Activity

"The Twelve Days of Story Time"
by Rob Reid
Sung to the tune of "The Twelve Days of Christmas."

Let the kids know that "'teller" is short for "storyteller."

On the first day of Story Time,
The 'teller shared with me,
A book about a curious monkey.

On the second day of Story Time,
The 'teller shared with me,
Two Dr. Seuss,
And a book about a curious monkey.

On the third day of Story Time,
The 'teller shared with me,
Three fingerplays,
Two Dr. Seuss,
And a book about a curious monkey.

On the fourth day of Story Time,
The 'teller shared with me,
Four funny poems,
Three fingerplays,
Two Dr. Seuss,
And a book about a curious monkey.

On the fifth day of Story Time,
The 'teller shared with me,
Five animal noises, *(Invite the audience members to make animal noises every time you reach this part of the verse.)*
Four funny poems,
Three fingerplays,
Two Dr. Seuss,
And a book about a curious monkey.

On the sixth day of Story Time,
The 'teller shared with me,
Six arts and crafts,
Five animal noises,
Four funny poems,
Three fingerplays,
Two Dr. Seuss,
And a book about a curious monkey.

On the seventh day of Story Time,
The 'teller shared with me,
Seven pop-up books,
Six arts and crafts,
Five animal noises,
Four funny poems,
Three fingerplays,
Two Dr. Seuss,
And a book about a curious monkey.

On the eighth day of Story Time,
The 'teller shared with me,
Eight sing-along songs,
Seven pop-up books,

Six arts and crafts,
Five animal noises,
Four funny poems,
Three fingerplays,
Two Dr. Seuss,
And a book about a curious monkey.

On the ninth day of Story Time,
The 'teller shared with me,
Nine nursery rhymes,
Eight sing-along songs,
Seven pop-up books,
Six arts and crafts,
Five animal noises,
Four funny poems,
Three fingerplays,
Two Dr. Seuss,
And a book about a curious monkey.

On the tenth day of Story Time,
The 'teller shared with me,
Ten Hokey-Pokey's,
Nine nursery rhymes,
Eight sing-along songs,
Seven pop-up books,
Six arts and crafts,
Five animal noises,
Four funny poems,
Three fingerplays,
Two Dr. Seuss,
And a book about a curious monkey.

On the eleventh day of Story Time,
The 'teller shared with me,
Eleven puppet shows,
Ten Hokey-Pokey's,
Nine nursery rhymes,
Eight sing-along songs,
Seven pop-up books,
Six arts and crafts,
Five animal noises,
Four funny poems,
Three fingerplays,
Two Dr. Seuss,
And a book about a curious monkey.

On the twelfth day of Story Time,
The 'teller shared with me,
Twelve yummy treats,

Eleven puppet shows,
Ten Hokey-Pokey's,
Nine nursery rhymes,
Eight sing-along songs,
Seven pop-up books,
Six arts and crafts,
Five animal noises,
Four funny poems,
Three fingerplays,
Two Dr. Seuss,
And a book about a curious monkey.

Movement Ideas for "The Twelve Days of Story Time"

If you're very adventurous, you can add "over-the-top" movements and sound effects for each line in the song. I found these additions work best with upper-elementary kids.

1. A book about a curious monkey: *Scratch head and armpits and go "Ooo ooo."*

2. Two Dr. Seuss: *Yell out "Green Eggs and Ham."*

3. Three fingerplays: *Hold hands up in the air and move fingers around.*

4. Four funny poems: *Laugh aloud.*

5. Five animal noises: *Continue to add animal noises.*

6. Six arts and crafts: *Mime using scissors, drawing, gluing, etc.*

7. Seven pop-up books: *Jump.*

8. Eight sing-along songs: *Hold out arms and go "La-la-la."*

9. Nine nursery rhymes: *Make hand motions for "The Itsy-Bitsy Spider" climbing.*

10. Ten Hokey-Pokey's: *Put one arm "in" and put one arm "out."*

11. Eleven puppet shows: *Jerk arms as if attached to strings like a marionette.*

12. Twelve yummy treats: *Rub tummy.*

Backup Picture Books

Amelia Bedelia, Bookworm by Herman Parish, illustrated by Lynn Sweat. Greenwillow Books, 2003. Amelia Bedelia hangs out at the local public library and comes up with new interpretations to common library phrases and terms. For example, when Amelia Bedelia hears that the books need jackets, she sews tiny jackets to slip over the books. Due to a misunderstanding, Amelia Bedelia "borrows" the bookmobile without proper permission from the librarian.

Beatrice Doesn't Want To by Laura Joffe Numeroff, illustrated by Lynn Munsinger. Candlewick Press, 2004. Beatrice dislikes books, reading, and going to the library. She's forced to go with her brother Henry, who is doing a report on dinosaurs. Beatrice constantly says, "I don't want to." She attends her first library story program and, of course, enjoys it. At the end of the book, when it's time for her to leave the library and go home, she says, "I don't want to." Ask your audience if they're ready to go home. Some will say yes and some will say, "I don't want to!"

I. Q. Goes to the Library by Mary Ann Fraser. Walker & Co., 2003. I. Q. the class pet rodent (mouse? gerbil?) goes along with the class to visit the school's library. He learns about stories, the different categories of books and recordings, and computers. He designs his own permission slip to get a library card, which the teacher happily signs.

The Librarian from the Black Lagoon by Mike Thaler, illustrated by Jared Lee. Scholastic, 1997. The kids worry about going to the school library. The rumor is that Mrs. Beamster, the librarian, is mean. She doesn't let kids stay longer than they can hold their breath. She bolts the books to the shelves. She glues kids to their chairs. She keeps Venus Flytraps and piranhas in the library, and even has a real mouse at the computer! Once the class arrives at the real library, they find it to be a very cool place.

Please Bury Me in the Library by J. Patrick Lewis, illustrated by Kyle M. Stone. Harcourt, 2005. Lewis includes 15 original poems that celebrate libraries, books, and reading. Titles include "If Books Had Different Names," "Eating Alphabet Soup," "Reading in the Dark," and "Summer Reading at the Beach."

Old (And Not So Old) Favorites

Aunt Lulu by Daniel Pinkwater. Macmillan, 1988.

Clemen's Kingdom by Chris Demarest. Lothrop, Lee & Shepard, 1983.

The Day the TV Blew Up by Dan West, illustrated by Gioia Fiammenghi. Albert Whitman, 1988.

How My Library Grew, by Dinah by Martha Alexander. Wilson, 1983.

The Library by Sarah Stewart, illustrated by David Small. Farrar, Straus, and Giroux, 1995.

Molly at the Library by Ruth Radlauer, illustrated by Emily Arnold McCully. Prentice-Hall, 1988.

Walter's Magic Wand by Eric Houghton, illustrated by Denise Teasdale. Orchard Books, 1989.

Why Did the Chicken Cross the Road?

As the audience enters the program area, play the chicken medley from Sharon, Lois, and Bram's recording *Sing A to Z* (Elephant Records, 1990). The lively medley includes the songs "C-H-I-C-K-E-N," "Chick, Chick, Chicken," and "Ham and Eggs." Once everyone is seated, ask the chapter title question "Why DID the chicken cross the road?" After listening to a variety of responses from the children, tell them the real answer is "Because she wanted to go to Storytime!" and launch right into your first picture book.

Picture Book

Crabby Cratchitt by Gregory Maguire, illustrated by Andrew Glass. Clarion Books, 2000. This rhythmic text about an old woman and her annoying hen begins "Crabby Cratchitt had a farm, / E-I-E-I-oh / And on that farm she had a hen, / E-I-E-I-oh." It's hard not to sing this humorous story (even though the text strays from the "Old MacDonald" format). The constant clucking drives Crabby crazy. After a fox attack, the hen is traumatized and stops clucking. Crabby realizes how much she misses the constant noise and does something about it.

Poem with Props

"A Little Talk"
Anonymous

This is a good poem to recite with the aid of puppets, stuffed toys, or felt images of a chicken and a duck.

> The big brown hen and Mrs. Duck,
> Went walking out together;
> They talked about all sorts of things—
> The farmyard and the weather.

But all I heard was:
"Cluck! Cluck! Cluck!"
And "Quack! Quack! Quack!"
From Mrs. Duck.

You can extend this activity with other farm animals. For example:

The big pink pig and Mrs. Sheep,
Went walking out together;
They talked about all sorts of things—
The farmyard and the weather.

But all I heard was:
"Oink! Oink! Oink!"
And "Baa! Baa! Baa!"
From Mrs. Sheep.

Picture Book

Old Mr. Mackle Hackle by Gunnar Madsen, illustrated by Irana Shepherd. Little, Brown, and Company, 2005. "Old Mr. Mackle Hackle had a hen that wouldn't cackle." The hen squeaks and quacks. He tells a plethora of bad chicken jokes: "If your chicken lays an egg on top of the barn, what do you get? An egg roll." Old Mr. Mackle Hackle eventually learns the chicken can talk like humans. She lays several eggs that hatch chicks that cackle all day long. This picture book is based on an original song by the author.

Fingerplay

"Ten Chicken Eggs"
Traditional

Five eggs, *(Hold up five fingers.)*
And five eggs, *(Hold up five more fingers.)*

That makes … ten.
(Pause and let the children answer "Ten!")
Sitting on top is,
Mother Hen. *(Place fist on other hand.)*

Crackle! Crackle! Crackle! *(Clap three times.)*
What do I see? *(Look amazed.)*
Ten fluffy chicks,
(Hold up ten fingers and wiggle them.)
As yellow as can be. *(Close fists.)*

Peep! Peep! Peep! Peep!
(Hold up a finger for each peep.)
Peep! Peep! Peep! Peep!
Peep! Peep!

Picture Book

Dora's Chicks by Julie Sykes, illustrated by Jane Chapman. Tiger Tales, 2002. Dora's six chicks disappear while she's out getting breakfast. She asks the various barnyard mothers if they've seen her chicks, but they've been busy watching after their own offspring. Dora manages to find her chicks one by one as they mingle and imitate the habits of the other farm animals.

Movement Activity

"Dance Like a Chicken"
Anonymous

Have the children stand and move around in small circles while bobbing their heads and "flapping their wings."

Everybody do the chicken dance.
Dance like there's ants in your pants,
And do the chicken dance.

An old, old man from down the street,
Sat on a bench and tapped his feet.
He stood up and gave me a glance,
And then he did the Chicken Dance.

Everybody do the chicken dance.
Dance like there's ants in your pants,
And do the chicken dance.

A leprechaun came up to me,
And asked "Where would my Ireland be?"
I said "Cross the sea and take a chance,
But before you go do the chicken dance!"

Everybody do the chicken dance.
Dance like there's ants in your pants,
And do the chicken dance.

There was a lot of noise coming from town,
Everyone I saw was jumping up and down.
They seemed to be in a funny trance,
They were all doing the chicken dance!

Everybody do the chicken dance.
Dance like there's ants in your pants,
And do the chicken dance.

Picture Book

Tippy-Toe Chick, Go! by George Shannon, illustrated by Laura Dronzek. Greenwillow Books, 2003. Little Chick shows her Mama, Big Chick, and Middle Chick how to get past "a big, grumpy dog" and over to the "sweet itty-bitty beans and potato bugs." Have fun reading the dog's ferocious series of "RUFF-RUFF-RUFF-RUFF-RUFF" followed by "yip-yip-yip" when Little Chick tricks the dog into wrapping himself with his own leash.

Movement Activity

"Tippy, Tippy, Tippytoe"
Traditional

Have the children stand and walk on their "tippytoes" in a line around the program area as you recite this ditty.

Tippy, Tippy, Tippytoe,
There they go,
Several little baby chicks,
Walking in a row.

They couldn't find a thing to eat,
And so they had to go,
Tippy, Tippy, Tippytoe,
Tippy, Tippy, Tippytoe,
Tippy, Tippy, Tippytoe.

Musical Activity

"The Chicken Dance"
Traditional

Here's the dance that many folks know and perform at various functions. The Web site (www. allmusic.com) lists 65 different recordings that have "The Chicken Dance." Here's a brief list:

- *Disney's Dance-Along.* Disney, 1997.
- *Dora the Explorer.* Nick Records, 2004.
- *Favorite Children's Songs.* Sony, 2004.

Play the music and instruct the children to perform the following motions:

First sequence: *Open and close hands like chicken beaks four times.*

Second sequence: *Flap arms like chicken wings four times.*

Third sequence: *Wiggle hips like chicken tails and bend at the knees.*

Fourth sequence: *Clap four times.*

Have the children do these motions as they leave the program area. Mostly, their parents and caregivers will greet them and spontaneously join in.

Backup Picture Books

Chicken in the Kitchen by Tony Johnston, illustrated by Eleanor Taylor. Simon & Schuster, 2005. An anthropomorphic dog is upset about the restless chicken in her kitchen. "… she's pokin' like the dickens at the oven and the bread box. Just a peckin' and a pickin'." Eventually, the dog realizes that the hen needs help making a nest. Soon, the dog has "a whole kitchen full of chickens!"

Cluck, Cluck, Who's There? by James Mayhew, illustrated by Caroline Jayne Church. Scholastic, 2004. This simple lift-the-flap book describes a hen with three eggs that hatch into three chicks. The flaps open up to reveal first the eggs and then the hidden chicks tucked beneath the hen's wings.

Cluck O'Clock by Kes Gray, illustrated by Mary McQuillan. Holiday House, 2004. The story begins at four o'clock in the morning and follows several chickens as they go through their day. They lay white or brown eggs (one chicken does requests), stroll through the farmyard, hunt for worms,

dive-bomb the ducks, find shapes in the clouds, and more. Later that evening (at precisely 10:57), they worry about Olga the fox. When the fox eventually leaves the area, it's 12 o'clock midnight and time for sleep.

Cock-a-Moo-Moo by Juliet Dallas-Conté, illustrated by Alison Bartlett. Little, Brown, and Company, 2001. Rooster forgets how to crow. Instead, he goes Cock-a-Moo-Moo, Cock-a-Quack-Quack, Cock-a-Oink-Oink, and Cock-a-Baa-Baa. When a fox creeps into the henhouse, Rooster lets loose with a cacophony of mixed-up calls, which alert the other animals to chase the fox away. The kids in the audience will most likely try to correct the rooster when he gives the wrong calls.

Goodnight Lulu by Paulette Bogan. Bloomsbury, 2003. Lulu, a young chicken, worries at bedtime. She wonders what will happen if a bear, a tiger, and an alligator come into her room at night while she sleeps. Momma assures Lulu that she'll drag the bear back to the forest, the tiger back to the jungle, and the alligator back to the swamp. When Lulu asks what will happen if pigs come in at night (two pigs have been watching this exchange the whole time), Momma says, "Then I would grab them and squeeze them and kiss them all over their faces!" The two pigs happily join Lulu in her nest.

Hoppity Skip Little Chick by Jo Brown. Tiger Tales, 2005. Little Chick has an adventurous day by running with some geese, bouncing with a lamb, jumping with a horse, and rolling around on the ground with a piglet. When Little Chick returns to the henhouse, he finds new siblings who are ready to play "hopping-running-rolling-skipping games for the rest of the day."

Hungry Hen by Richard Waring, illustrated by Caroline Jayne Church. HarperCollins, 2001. This picture book is basically a single joke with a silly punch line. A little hen eats and eats and eats. The more she eats, the more she grows. A fox watches her get bigger and bigger. He plots to eat her when she reaches the perfect size. Finally, he decides that the hen is ready to be eaten. "… Just as the fox was ready to pounce … the hen bent down—and gobbled him all up!"

Queenie, One of the Family by Bob Graham. Candlewick Press, 1997. A human family (and their dog Bruno) rescues a hen from drowning in a pond and takes her home. They name her Queenie. She quickly becomes "one of the family." The family finds Queenie's true home on a farm and returns her. However, Queenie makes the long trek back to their house each day for several days to lay eggs. Eventually, Queenie stays on the farm, but now the family (and their dog Bruno) own several chicks.

Silly Chicken by Rukhsana Khan, illustrated by Yunmee Kyong. Viking, 2005. Set in rural Pakistan, a little girl named Rani is jealous of a chicken. She feels as if her mother loves Bibi the chicken more than her. Rani thinks the chicken is so silly, it doesn't even know how to properly lay an egg. Rani is blamed when Bibi goes missing. Bibi never returns, but her egg hatches.

Rani becomes enamored with the chick she names "Bibi Ki Buchi. It means Bibi's child. But we call her Buchi for short."

Old (And Not So Old) Favorites

Across the Stream by Mirra Ginsburg, illustrated by Nancy Tafuri. Greenwillow Books, 1982.

The Chick and the Duckling by V. Suteyev, translated by Mirra Ginsburg, illustrated by Jose Aruego and Ariane Dewey. Macmillan, 1972.

Chicken Little by Steven Kellogg. William Morrow & Co., 1985.

Good Morning, Chick by Mirra Ginsburg, illustrated by Byron Barton. Greenwillow Books, 1980.

Hattie and the Fox by Mem Fox, illustrated by Patricia Mullins. Bradbury, 1986.

Henny Penny by Paul Galdone. Houghton Mifflin, 1968.

Little Red Hen by Paul Galdone. Houghton Mifflin, 1973.

Minerva Louise by Janet Morgan Stoeke. Dutton Children's Books, 1988.

Wings: A Tale of Two Chickens by James Marshall. Houghton Mifflin, 1986.

The Wolf's Chicken Stew by Keiko Kasza. Putnam, 1987.

Zinnia and Dot by Lisa Campbell Ernst. Viking, 1992.